Introduction to Chinese Natural Language Processing

Synthesis Lectures on Human Language Technologies

Editor

Graeme Hirst, University of Toronto

Synthesis Lectures on Human Language Technologies publishes monographs on topics relating to natural language processing, computational linguistics, information retrieval, and spoken language understanding. Emphasis is placed on important new techniques, on new applications, and on topics that combine two or more HLT subfields.

Introduction to Chinese Natural Language Processing
Kam-Fai Wong, Wenjie Li, Ruifeng Xu, Zheng-sheng Zhang
2010

Introduction to Linguistic Annotation and Text Analytics
Graham Wilcock
2009

Dependency Parsing
Sandra Kübler, Ryan McDonald, Joakim Nivre
2009

Statistical Language Models for Information Retrieval
ChengXiang Zhai
2008

Introduction to Chinese Natural Language Processing
Kam-Fai Wong, Wenjie Li, Ruifeng Xu, and Zheng-sheng Zhang

ISBN: 978-3-031-01005-7   paperback

ISBN: 978-3-031-02133-6   ebook

DOI: 10.1007/978-3-031-02133-6

A Publication in the Springer series

SYNTHESIS LECTURES ON HUMAN LANGUAGE TECHNOLOGIES

Lecture #4

Series Editor: Graeme Hirst, University of Toronto

Series ISSN

ISSN 1947-4040 print

ISSN 1947-4059 electronic

Introduction to Chinese Natural Language Processing

Kam-Fai Wong
Chinese University of Hong Kong

Wenjie Li
Hong Kong Polytechnic University

Ruifeng Xu
City University of Hong Kong

Zheng-sheng Zhang
San Diego State University

SYNTHESIS LECTURES ON HUMAN LANGUAGE TECHNOLOGIES # 4

ABSTRACT

This book introduces Chinese language-processing issues and techniques to readers who already have a basic background in natural language processing (NLP). Since the major difference between Chinese and Western languages is at the word level, the book primarily focuses on Chinese morphological analysis and introduces the concept, structure, and interword semantics of Chinese words.

The following topics are covered: a general introduction to Chinese NLP; Chinese characters, morphemes, and words and the characteristics of Chinese words that have to be considered in NLP applications; Chinese word segmentation; unknown word detection; word meaning and Chinese linguistic resources; interword semantics based on word collocation and NLP techniques for collocation extraction.

KEYWORDS

Chinese processing, natural language processing, morphological analysis

Contents

CHAPTER 1

Introduction

The world is flat [Friedman 2005]. Globalization has virtually lifted the boundaries between countries. Apparently, the advancement of the Internet is an active catalyst of the globalization process. Today, the World Wide Web (WWW) is no longer dominated by English-speaking surfers. In 2008, 29.4% (i.e., 4.3×10^8) of the world's Internet users communicate in English; this is second only to the number of Chinese-speaking users, who account for 18.9% (i.e., 2.8×10^8) [Internet World Stats 2007]. Since 2000, the latter has grown by 755%, and this trend has shown no sign of diminishing.

Businesspeople worldwide are actively studying the Internet in order to achieve customer relationship management (CRM) to better serve their multiracial and multicultural customers. Similarly, governments are doing the same to better serve their citizens. Internet-based CRM [often referred to as electronic CRM (e-CRM)] extensively employs natural language processing (NLP) techniques to analyze the content of the Web in different languages. Due to the growing Chinese market, more and more e-business portals include Chinese information. For this reason, there is a growing demand in Chinese NLP research and development.

1.1 WHAT IS CHINESE NLP?

A language is a dynamic set of symbols and the corresponding rules for visual, auditory, tactile, or textual communication. Human languages are usually referred to as natural languages; the science of studying natural languages falls under the purview of linguistics, and its implementation using computational means is regarded as computational linguistics. While computational linguistics focuses on theoretical aspects of human languages using computers, NLP can be considered as a technique for the realization of linguistic theory to facilitate real-world applications, e.g., online content analysis for e-CRM, machine translation, information extraction, document summarization. NLP is performed in three stages: morphological, syntactic, and semantic analyses. In addition, Chinese NLP is no exception.

Lack of clear delimiters between words in a Chinese sentence renders Chinese NLP unique from Western languages, e.g., English. For this reason, automatic word segmentation, the major step in Chinese morphological analysis, lays down the foundation of any modern Chinese information systems. For example, the following sequence of characters:

香港人口多
白天鹅已飞走了

can be easily segmented, i.e., to identify the legal words, by humans to form meaningful sentences, e.g.,

香港 人口 多 (The population of Hong Kong is large)
白天 鹅 已 飞走 了 (The goose has already flown away during the day)

However, it is not so straightforward for a computer to perform automatic word segmentation. Some word segmentation algorithm, e.g., the dictionary-based right-to-left maximum matching algorithm could lead to different interpretations for the above sequences, e.g.,

香港 人 口多 (Hong Kong people are talkative)
白 天鹅 已 飞走 了 (The white swan has already flown away)

Notice that segmentation of the character sequence 人口多 can result in two possible word sequences, namely, 人口 多 (population is large) and 人 口多 (people are talkative). In the other example, 白天鹅 can be interpreted as 白天 鹅 (goose during the day) or 白 天鹅 (white swan). To resolve ambiguity in word segmentation, one could adopt a rule-based algorithm, which incorporates grammatical or commonsense knowledge. For example, the above could be resolved by the following simple rules:

1. 人口 多 (population is large) is more common, as the phrase 口多 (talkative) is a slang term mostly used in Hong Kong only. Thus, the former is preferred.
2. 天鹅 (swan) can fly (飞), but 鹅 (goose) cannot. Thus, the former is preferred.

Both examples require supplementary linguistic resources for effective word segmentation. Although some of these resources are available, they are not in machine-readable form. This makes Chinese NLP difficult, if not impossible.

Following word segmentation, part-of-speech (POS) tagging is applied to the word sequence. This requires a POS dictionary, in which a word is associated with its POS tag(s). More than one tag to a word is common, e.g., 计划 (plan) is both a verb and a noun in Chinese. To decide which tag to use often depends on the position of the word in the sentence, e.g.,

他 划 去 香港 (He plans to go to Hong Kong)
去 香港 是 他 的 计划 (Going to Hong Kong is his plan)

where the former 计划 (plan) is used as a verb and the latter a noun. In fact, almost all bisyllabic Chinese words are associated with more than one POS tag, e.g., 建议 (suggest/suggestion), 鼓励 (encourage/encouragement), etc.

Based on the results of word segmentation and POS tagging, syntactic analysis develops the sentence structure, which is not the same as the linear sequence of the words, but rather it is structured hierarchically. Take the sentence 学会认为她是班长 as an example. After word segmentation and POS tagging, the linear word and POS sequences are as follows:

同学会 (n) 认为 (v) 她 (r) 是 (v) 班长 (n)

where n, v, and r are noun, verb, and pronoun, respectively. However, this linear structure is not useful for NLP. It is therefore transformed into a syntactic tree based on a set of predefined grammar rules and the corresponding parsing algorithm. For example, the above example would be parsed into the syntax tree shown in Figure 1.1. Similar to compilation of a computer program, this tree provides the core information structure for further computer processing. For example, a machine translation (MT) system will try to understand this structure and, based on its semantics, synthesize a sentence in the target language. For another example, an information retrieval system will extract the key concepts from this tree for indexing purposes.

It is noteworthy that this structure is developed based on the original linear POS sequence. POS sequence is more abstract than word sequence. Its linguistic coverage is relatively broader. For example, sentences such as 黄先生 (n) 知道 (v) 你 (r) 是 (v) 律师 (n) (Mr. Wong knows that you are a lawyer) and 政府 (n) 承认 (v) 他 (r) 是 (v) 专家 (n) (The government recognizes him as an expert) have the same parse tree structure. But consider the sentence 会 (n) 推选 (v) 他 (r) 当 (v)

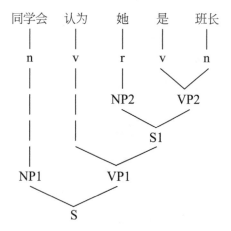

FIGURE 1.1: Syntactic tree example of "同学会 (n) 认为 (v) 她 (r) 是(v) 班长 (n)."

主席 (n), which shares a common linear POS sequence as the previous examples. Its tree structure, however, is different (Figure 1.2). This inevitably produces ambiguity at the syntactic analysis level. Additional information, such as grammatical and/or commonsense knowledge, is required for disambiguation, i.e., to select the appropriate tree structure from the two.

Aside from one linear POS sequence resulting in multiple tree structures, another form of ambiguity arises when one common tree structure results in multiple meanings. This lays down the primary objective of semantic analysis, i.e., to work out the meaning of the sentence, which is often not directly deducible from the given tree structure. Consider the sample sentences: 音乐家 (n) 打 (v) 鼓 (n) (The musician plays the drum), 妈妈 (n) 打 (v) 麻将 (n) (Mother plays mahjong), and 运动员 (n) 打 (v) 网球 (n) (The sportsman plays tennis). All three sentences share the same tree structure (see Figure 1.3).

How could an NLP system extract the meaning of these three sentences? This is practically impossible by simply analyzing the given tree structure. In fact, there are some hidden semantic clues behind the sentence, which could be used to resolve the ambiguity. Notice that the verb of these three sentences is the same, namely, 打; however, its associated subjects are different, namely, 音乐家 (musician), 妈妈 (mother), and 运动员 (sportsman), respectively. Nevertheless, if a semantic dictionary, which entails the following entries:

- play1 (musicians, instruments), i.e., musicians play instruments, and a drum is an instrument,
- play2 (mothers, household games), i.e., mothers play household games, and mahjong is a household game, and
- play3 (sportsmen, sport), i.e., sportsmen play sports, and tennis is a sport,

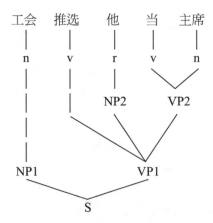

FIGURE 1.2: Syntactic tree example of "工会 (n) 推选 (v) 他 (r) 当 (v) 主席 (n)."

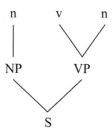

FIGURE 1.3: Common syntactic tree for the following sentences: 音乐家 (n) 打 (v) 鼓 (n) (The musician plays the drum), 妈妈 (n) 打 (v) 麻将 (n) (Mother plays mahjong), and 运动员 (n) 打 (v) 网球 (n) (The sportsman plays tennis).

were available, the system would be able to understand the semantics of these sentences better. Semantic knowledge resources are the prerequisites of this stage of NLP. However, compared with English and other Western languages, such resources for Chinese NLP are relatively fewer. As a result, many researchers, particularly in mainland China and Taiwan, are working actively and diligently to develop different Chinese linguistic resources.

The main difference in NLP for Chinese and other languages takes place in the first stage. This lays down the objective of this book, namely, to introduce the basic techniques in Chinese morphological analysis.

1.2 ABOUT THIS BOOK

This book focuses on Chinese morphological analysis, which is the basic building block of Chinese NLP. It is divided into three parts: concept (Chapters 2 and 3), automatic identification (Chapters 4 and 5), and semantics (Chapters 6, 7, and 8) of Chinese words.

Chapter 2 presents the concepts of Chinese characters, morphemes, and words from a linguistic angle, and Chapter 3 outlines the characteristics of Chinese words worth considering by NLP applications. They lay down the foundation of later chapters. In Chapter 4, the problems and technical solutions of word segmentation are introduced. This is followed by the topic of unknown word detection in Chapter 5. Chapter 6 introduces the concept of word meaning and gives examples of several Chinese linguistic resources, which entail information about meanings of words and relationship between words. Lastly, Chapters 7 and 8 present the idea of interword semantics based on collocation of words and NLP techniques for collocation extraction, respectively.

· · · · ·

CHAPTER 2

Words in Chinese

2.1 INTRODUCTION

Since this book is on the morphological processing of Chinese, the following fundamental questions need to be addressed first:

- How are words represented in Chinese?
- How are words formed in Chinese?
- How can words be identified in Chinese?

While word formation in Chinese is not totally dissimilar from that in other languages, it is nonetheless distinct in the predominance of the morphological process of compounding and the relative paucity of affixation. Moreover, Chinese also employs the rather unusual morphological process of reduplication.

Word identification also poses special challenges for NLP in Chinese, mostly due to the unusual Chinese writing system. In English and most other languages, a spoken word is represented in writing by a string of letters delimited on both sides by white spaces. In Chinese, however, we cannot identify words in a similar fashion, because in Chinese writing, no white spaces are left between units of the written script. Therefore, before morphological processing can take place, an addition step of segmentation is necessary, by which continuous strings of characters are cut into word chunks.

The unusual Chinese writing system and its writing convention also makes it more of a necessity to distinguish the units of writing, i.e., characters from those of the spoken language, i.e., morphemes and words, which are the relevant units for morphological processing.

2.2 CHARACTERS, MORPHEMES, AND WORDS
2.2.1 Characters (字)

The most salient feature of the Chinese script, which has important consequences for NLP of Chinese, is its non-alphabetic symbols, known as characters or 汉字 (written in Chinese characters). Visually, unlike the letters in alphabetic writing systems, the elements of Chinese characters are not arranged in a linear fashion but in the shape of a square block known as 方块字 (square characters). An example is 国 (*country*). Every character takes up the same amount of space.

Despite its pictographic origin and popular belief, the Chinese script, unusual as it is, is not for the most part pictographic. There are only a very small number of pictographs. Some familiar examples of pictographs are 日 (sun), 月 (moon), 水 (water), 火 (fire), and 人 (person). Similarly, there are very few characters that are ideographic, i.e., conveying ideas directly. They include simple indicative (指事) characters, such as 上 (up), 下 (down), 一 (one), 二 (two), 三 (three); and compound indicative (会意) characters such as 仁 (benevolence, =person+two), 信 (trust, =person+word), etc. Instead, over 90% of Chinese characters are semantic–phonetic compounds (形声) consisting of a phonetic component (声旁) representing sound and a semantic component (形旁), whose vague meaning serves to differentiate similar sounding homophones rather than giving concrete indication of meaning. Some examples of semantic–phonetic compounds are 请, 情, 清, 晴, which all share the phonetic component 青 (pronounced as *qing*) but differ in having the word, heart, water, and sun semantic component, respectively. Therefore, although the sound of many characters can be deduced from the phonetic component, the meanings of characters for the most part cannot be deduced from either the shapes or the composition of characters.

Functionally, unlike the letters in alphabetic systems, Chinese characters do not represent individual phonemes. Instead, according to DeFrancis [1984], Chinese writing is morphosyllabic, i.e., each Chinese character represents a single syllable that is also a minimal meaning-bearing unit of morpheme, a linguistic unit to be explained below.

Although text processing cannot avoid dealing with characters, it should be made clear that these symbols of writing cannot be equated with units of language. The symbols used in writing systems, characters in the case of Chinese, are not themselves units of language. As the present volume is mainly concerned with the morphological processing of Chinese text, the relevant linguistic units are the morphological units of morphemes (词素) and words (词). It is important to distinguish these units of spoken language from the characters (字) in the writing system. While characters have sociological and psychological salience and it is easy to visually identify them, they are not equivalent to words and morphemes, whose identification has to be based on semantic and syntactic grounds. While most Chinese characters represent single syllables, morphemes and words, however, can be of varying length, from the one-syllable 山 (mountain) to a four-syllable transliterated word 密西西比 (Mississippi).

2.2.2 Morphemes (词素)

The basic morphological units, i.e., the smallest meaningful elements, are called morphemes, which can be combined to form words. Being the smallest meaningful element, a morpheme cannot be further analyzed into smaller parts and still retain meaning. For example, in the English sentence *the company owns many properties*, three of the words—*the, company*, and *many*—each has only one morpheme, not being analyzable any further. But the two words *owns* and *properties* can each be cut into two morphemes. While *owns* consists of *own* and the third person singular ending *-s, properties* contains *property* and the plural ending *-s* (identical in sound to the third person singular *-s!*). As can be seen, a morpheme can have more than one syllable (e.g., *many, property*) or less than one syllable (e.g., the two *-s* morphemes) in English.

In contrast, most Chinese morphemes are monosyllabic. And each morpheme/syllable is written with one character. There are, however, exceptions to the generalization that one syllable is one morpheme represented by one character. For example, the following single-morpheme words all have more than one syllable: 葡萄 (grape), 菩萨 (Buddha), 马虎 (perfunctory), 马达 (motor), 咖啡 (coffee), 萨其马 (a kind of pastry), and 巧克力 (chocolate). Even though the syllables are written with characters that are meaningful elsewhere, in these words they are simply used to represent sounds. The meanings of these characters have nothing to do with the meanings of the word. Therefore, all these words have only one morpheme each. These words are exceptional in that they are loanwords from other languages. Native Chinese words are still largely true to the one-syllable–one-morpheme–one-character generalization.

2.2.3 Words (词)

The word is distinct from both morphemes at a lower level and from phrases at a higher level. The independence of the morphological unit of word can be justified both on grounds of distribution restriction and lexical integrity.

Distributional restriction. While a word can occur freely by itself (such as in one-word answers), a morpheme may or may not be able to. When a morpheme can occur by itself, it is a word with a single *free* morpheme; however, when a morpheme cannot occur by itself, it is called a *bound* morpheme and has to be combined with other morphemes to form a word. In the English example earlier, neither the plural *-s* nor the third person singular *-s* is a free morpheme; they are bound to a noun and a verb, respectively. Examples of bound morphemes in Chinese are also easy to find. All the grammatical morphemes, such as 的, 地, 得, 了, 着, 过, are bound, as they cannot occur by themselves. Some content morphemes are also bound, e.g., 行 (walk) and 饮 (drink). Although free in classical Chinese, they can no longer occur by themselves in modern Chinese and can only occur in words like 行人 (pedestrian), 行动 (action), 冷饮 (cold drink), and 饮料 (beverage).

Integrity of word meanings. Along with relatively greater syntactic freedom, words also have meanings that are not predictable from the meanings of their component morphemes. For example, the meaning of the word *blackboard* is not the same as the combination of its component morphemes may suggest in that a blackboard may or may not be black. Similarly, 大人 (adult) is not the same as 大的人 (big person), as you can say 小大人 (little adult, i.e., adult-like child). Nor is 小人

the same as 小的人; the former means a "petty/lowly person," whereas the latter refers to a "small person." The semantic relationship within words can also be distinct from that between words, namely, at the phrasal level. The phrase 打人 (beat+people) is a verb+object phrase meaning to beat people, but the word 打手 (beat+hand) does not mean to beat hand but is actually a noun referring to a hired thug/hatchet man.

The favored status of disyllabic words. One of the "myths" about Chinese is that it is a monosyllabic language, meaning its words are all one-syllable long. In his book *Chinese Language: Fact and Fantasy*, DeFrancis [1984] argued convincingly against such a myth. On the other hand, Chao [1968] noted that the monosyllabic myth may be the truest myth about Chinese. Monosyllabicity is either truth or myth, depending on whether the word or the morpheme is being considered. The overwhelming majority of Chinese morphemes are indeed one-syllable long. The morphemes that are multisyllabic only constitute 11% of the total number of morphemes. Hence, monosyllabicity is largely true of Chinese morphemes. On the other hand, only 44% of (monosyllabic) morphemes can occur by themselves as words. Therefore, monosyllabicity is not true of Chinese words.

Most Chinese words in fact have two syllables. In addition to various statistical figures, a number of facts point to the tendency toward the favored status of disyllabic expressions [Lü 1963]:

> ➤ The existence of disyllabic compounds whose component morphemes have the same meanings. For example, both of the morphemes in 保护 mean "protect;" both the morphemes in 购买 mean "buy," and both of the morphemes in 销售 mean "sell," etc. The extra syllable/morpheme seems not motivated on grounds of meaning.

> ➤ Most abbreviations (there are many in Chinese) are two-syllable long. Examples abound: Beijing Daxue (Peking University)→Beida.

> ➤ Monosyllabic place names need to be used with their category identifier such as 法国 (France=French+country), 英国 (England=English+country), 通县 (tong county), 涿县 (zhuo county), etc.; however, disyllabic names need not have such identifiers, e.g., 日本 (Japan), 印度 (India), 大兴 (Daxing), 顺义 (Shunyi), etc. Numbers are similar. Monosyllabic numbers like 1 through 10 have to go with their measure, e.g., 一号 (first), 十号 (10th), but disyllabic numbers need not, e.g., 十一 (11).

There is an interesting pattern in the use of Chinese names for terms of address. Chinese surnames are either one- or two-syllable long, and the given name is also one- or two-syllable long. Therefore, Chinese names can be two- to four-syllable long. An important consideration when addressing someone is politeness toward or familiarity with the person being addressed. An interesting pattern that emerges is that all the preferred choices and combinations add up to two syllables, sometimes overriding the politeness/familiarity consideration. So if only a monosyllabic surname is used, then a respectful or endearing prefix, such as 老 (old) or 小 (little), has to be added to the surname, e.g., 小李 (junior Li) or 老李 (senior Li). But if a disyllabic surname is used, no such prefix can be added, e.g., 欧阳 (Ouyang) or 端木 (Duanmu). If the given name is used, then one of two things can also happen. If the given name is disyllabic, then only the given name is used; but if the given name is monosyllabic and the surname is also monosyllabic, then the full name is used instead.

2.3   WORD FORMATION IN CHINESE

Word formation in Chinese is distinguished by the relative predominance of compounding compared with other morphological processes such as affixation and reduplication. Compounding is to combine root morphemes to form new words. While compounding is found in English as well, e.g., in the creation of the compound *sabertooth* from the words *saber* and *tooth*, compounding is much more prevalent in Chinese. The propensity for compounds is most obvious when monosyllabic words in English are expressed in Chinese by disyllabic compounds:

ENGLISH	CHINESE	COMPONENTS
Man	男人	Male+person
Woman	女人	Female+person
Merchant	商人	Commerce+person
Pork	猪肉	Pig+meat
Beef	牛肉	Cow+meat
Mutton	羊肉	Sheep+meat
Car	汽车	Air+vehicle
Train	火车	Fire+vehicle
Tram	电车	Electricity+vehicle

It is thus obvious that instead of creating totally new words, Chinese uses morphemes already existent in the language, such as 人 (man), 肉 (meat), and 车 (vehicle), to form compounds referring to different kinds of people, meat, and vehicles, respectively. Take the case of vehicles. New words for different kinds of vehicles are formed by using modifiers like 汽 (air), 火 (fire), and 电 (electricity) in front of the general morpheme 车 (vehicle).

2.3.1   Disyllabic Compounds

Although compounds can be formed from more than two morphemes, disyllabic compounds are the most important. This is not only because of their large number; it is also because of the fact that they can be building blocks for forming longer compounds. Hence, more of our attention will be given to disyllabic compounds.

Disyllabic compounds can be classified according to the structural relationships between the component morphemes.

1. *Modified noun compounds.* They constitute over 53% of all bimorphemic compounds. They have descriptive modifiers in front of nouns, even though the meaning of the whole is different from the simple addition of the meanings of the parts. They are like the *blackboard* cases in English.

EXAMPLES	MEANINGS OF COMPONENTS	MEANING OF COMPOUND
小人	Small+person	Mean/petty person
大人	Big+person	Adult
热心	Hot+heart	Warm-hearted
水手	Water+hand	Sailor
打手	Hit+hand	Thug
黑板	Black+board	Blackboard
去年	Go+year	Last year
爱人	Love+person	Spouse (mainland China)

2. *Modified verb compounds.* They have modifiers in front of verbs, specifying the manner in which the verbal action is carried out. They are like the *deep-fry* cases in English.

EXAMPLES	MEANINGS OF COMPONENTS	MEANING OF COMPOUND
寄生	Deposit+live	Live as parasite
飞驰	Fly+gallop	Speed along
杂居	Mix+live	Ethnically mixed living
火葬	Fire+bury	Cremate
面授	Face+impart	Instruct face to face
单恋	Single+love	Love in one direction

3. *Coordinative compounds.* The two morphemes in these compounds are equivalent in their function and account for over 27% of the bimorphemic compounds. They come in two subvarieties: synonymous compounds and antonymous compounds.

a) Synonymous compounds: the two-component morphemes have similar or identical meanings. There do not seem to be English equivalents.

EXAMPLES	MEANINGS OF COMPONENTS	MEANING OF COMPOUND
报告	Report+report	Report
声音	Sound+sound	Sound
奇怪	Strange+strange	Strange
刚才	Just now+just now	Just now
购买	Buy+buy	Purchase
销售	Sell+sell	Sell
学习	Study+practice	Study
帮助	Help+assist	Help

b) Antonymous compounds: the component morphemes have either opposite or contrary meanings. In addition to the obvious differences in meanings between the wholes and their parts, the parts of speech of the whole can also be different from its parts. This forms a clear contrast with the synonymous compounds above. There do not seem to be English equivalents.

EXAMPLES	MEANINGS OF COMPONENTS	MEANING OF COMPOUND
买卖	Buy+sell	Transaction
左右	Left+right	Approximately
高矮	Tall+short	Height
大小	Big+small	Size
开关	Open+shut	Switch
长短	Long+short	Length
轻重	Light+heavy	Weight
厚薄	Thick+thin	Thickness

4. *Verb–object compounds.* They consist of a verbal morpheme followed by an object morpheme and account for over 13% of the bimorphemic compounds. They can be either verbal or nominal, as the following two sets of examples illustrate, respectively:

Examples of verbal verb–object disyllabic compounds

EXAMPLES	MEANINGS OF COMPONENTS	MEANING OF COMPOUND
放心	Put down+heart	Rest assured, relax
鼓掌	Drum+palm	Clap
动员	Move+personnel	Mobilize

Examples of nominal verb–object disyllabic compounds

EXAMPLES	MEANINGS OF COMPONENTS	MEANING OF COMPOUND
司机	Manage+machine	Driver
主席	Primary+chair	Chairman
干事	Do+thing	Clerk
司仪	Manage+ceremony	Master of ceremony

5. *Verb complement compounds.* In these compounds, the verbal morpheme is followed by a complement [resultative verbal complement (RVC)] indicating either the direction or the result of the verbal process.

a)   Compounds with directional complements:

EXAMPLES	MEANINGS OF COMPONENTS	MEANING OF COMPOUND
进来	Enter+come	Come in
进去	Enter+go	Go in
介入	Introduce+enter	Interfere
超出	Supersede+out	Exceed

b)   Verb-resultative compounds. In these compounds, the verbal morpheme is followed by a RVC indicating the result of the verbal process. The need for RVC is dictated by the fact that Chinese verbal morphemes only encode the action phase but not the result phase. Thus a verbal morpheme like 看 only conveys the meaning of looking, without indicating whether the looking is finished or whether the looking has lead to perception. When there is need to convey the meaning that the action of looking not only has taken place but also has led to perception, an RVC like 见 (perceive) is necessary.

EXAMPLES	MEANINGS OF COMPONENTS	MEANING OF COMPOUND
改良	Change+good	Improve
打破	Hit+broken	Break
推翻	Push+over	Overthrow
看见	Look+perceive	See
听见	Listen+perceive	Hear
闻到	Sniff+perceive	Smell
煮熟	Cook+cooked	Cook
提高	Lift+high	Raise

There do not seem to be equivalents in English, which has a different strategy for expressing the result meaning of verbs. Instead of adding RVC to action-only verbs, it uses entirely new verbs, which encode both the action phase and the result phase. Therefore, there often exist doublets for the same action, one action only and the other with both action and result. The following three pairs are good illustrations:

ACTION ONLY	ACTION+RESULT
Look	See
Listen	Hear
Study	Learn

We can think of the words on the right as having a built-in RVC meaning, which is invisible on the surface. In this sense then, the meaning structure of Chinese verbal compounds is more transparent.

6. *Subject–predicate compounds.* The semantic relationship between their parts is analogous to that of a subject and a predicate (a verb or an adjective) in a sentence. They are like *earthquake* in English.

EXAMPLES	MEANINGS OF COMPONENTS	MEANING OF COMPOUND
地震	Ground+shake	Earthquake
心疼	Heart+ache	Feel something is wasted
民主	People+decide	Democracy
自决	Self+decide	Self-determination
胆小	Gallbladder+small	Timid
年轻	Year+light	Young
性急	Personality+urgent	Impatient
月亮	Moon+bright	Moon

7. *Noun-measure complement compounds.* There is another rather interesting type of disyllabic compound whose morphemes do not exhibit any of the usual grammatical relationships; in this kind of compounds, a noun is followed by a measure word complement to denote a generic kind that the noun is a member of.

EXAMPLES	MEANINGS OF COMPONENTS	MEANING OF COMPOUND
人口	Person+mouth (measure)	Population
羊群	Sheep+group (measure)	Flock of sheep
书本	Book+copy (measure)	Books

花朵	Flower+measure	Flowers
枪支	Gun+stick (measure)	Guns
车辆	Vehicle+measure	Vehicles

2.3.2   Trisyllabic Compounds

In such compounds, with the exception of cases like 亚非拉 (Asia Africa Latin America) whose three-component morphemes exhibit a coordinative relationship, the possibility of hierarchical structure arises. In a string of ABC, there can be closer grouping between AB or BC. When A and B are closer, the structure is left-branching, i.e., [AB] C; when B and C are closer, the structure is right-branching, i.e., A [BC]. The disyllabic strings that are closer together may in fact be freely occurring disyllabic words by themselves, but they may not always be. For example, in 口香糖 (mouth scent candy=chewing gum), even though 口香(mouth scented) are closer together, they cannot occur freely as a word elsewhere.

The greater number of syllables gives rise to the possibility of ambiguous analyses. For example, 大学生 can be analyzed, without looking beyond the word, either as 大/学生 or 大学/生, as both 学生 and 大学 are words.

As trisyllabic compounds can have disyllabic compounds embedded in them, the types of structural relationships found in these compounds being as varied as those in disyllabic compounds. The extra structural possibilities made possible by the additional syllable only add to the number of possible types. We will only give some examples of the most common types as well as those that are only possible with at least three syllables.

1. *Modifier–noun.* Compounds of this type constitute three-fourths of the total number.

EXAMPLES	MEANINGS OF MORPHEMES INTERNAL			
STRUCTURE	MEANINGS OF PARTS		MEANING OF WHOLE	
情人节	Emotion+man+ festival	[情人]节	[Lover] festival	Valentine's day

小说家	Small+speak+ specialist	[小说]家	[Novel] specialist	Novelist
加油站	Add+oil+station	[加油]站	[Oil filling] station	Gas station
大学生	Big+school+ student	[大学]生	[University] student	College student
金黄色	Gold+yellow+ color	[金黄]色	[Gold yellow] color	Golden color

2. *Verb–object*. They are the next most common type of trisyllabic compounds.

EXAMPLES	MEANINGS OF MORPHEMES	INTERNAL STRUCTURE	MEANING OF PARTS	MEANING OF WHOLE
开玩笑	Open+play+laugh	开[玩笑]	Do [joke]	To joke
吹牛皮	Blow+ox+skin	吹[牛皮]	Blow [ox skin]	To boast
吃豆腐	Eat+bean+curd	吃[豆腐]	Eat [tofu]	Take advantage of girls

3. *Subject–verb–object*. These compounds with three grammatical parts are naturally only possible with at least three syllables.

EXAMPLES	MEANINGS OF MORPHEMES	INTERNAL STRUCTURE	MEANING OF PARTS	MEANING OF WHOLE
胆结石	Gallbladder+ form+stone	胆[结石]	Gallbladder [form+stone]	Gallbladder stone
鬼画符	Ghost+draw+sign	鬼[画符]	Ghost [draw+sign]	Gibberish

4. *Descriptive+noun.* These compounds, with their reduplicative or onomatopoetic disyllables preceding the head noun, are unique to trisyllabic forms.

EXAMPLES	MEANINGS OF MORPHEMES	INTERNAL STRUCTURE	MEANING OF PARTS	MEANING OF WHOLE
棒棒糖	Stick+stick+candy	[棒棒]糖	Stick candy	Lollipop
乒乓球	Ping+pong+ball	[乒乓]球	Ping pong ball	Pingpong ball
呼啦圈	Hoo+la+hoop	[呼啦]圈	Hoola hoop	Hoola hoop

2.3.3   Quadrasyllabic Compounds

One type of compounds with four syllables is of course those built from disyllable components, exemplified by the following, with pairs of synonymous disyllable compounds conjoined.

EXAMPLES	MEANINGS OF MORPHEMES	INTERNAL STRUCTURE	MEANING OF WHOLE
骄傲自满	Proud haughty self full	[骄傲][自满]	Full of oneself
艰难困苦	Hard difficult difficult hard	[艰难][困苦]	Hard and difficult
铺张浪费	Spread open willful waste	[铺张][浪费]	Wasteful
粗心大意	Thick heart big intent	[粗心][大意]	Careless

As these compounds are built from disyllabic components, they can exhibit all the structural relationships possible with disyllabic compounds. We will not enumerate the different types here; instead, we will focus on some special types only possible with four syllable compounds.

Chinese has a huge number of fixed expressions with four syllables. The patterns for the formation of these expressions are astoundingly varied. They cannot all be generated with simple conjoining of disyllable compounds. Instead, they are formed by a process referred to as *interweaving*. Synonymous and antonymous pairs are interwoven with numbers, directional morphemes, and reduplicated elements. Some commonly encountered types are enlisted below:

–   pairs of synonyms interwoven

EXAMPLES	MEANINGS OF MORPHEMES	MEANING OF WHOLE
花言巧语	Flower word fine speech	Sweet talk
油腔滑调	Oil accent slippery tone	Glib/smooth talking

–   pairs of antonyms interwoven

EXAMPLES	MEANINGS OF MORPHEMES	MEANING OF WHOLE
大同小异	Big same small different	Basically the same
口是心非	Mouth yes heart no	Duplicitous
阳奉阴违	Open obey hidden disobey	Duplicitous

–   pairs of synonyms and antonyms interwoven

EXAMPLES	MEANINGS OF MORPHEMES	MEANING OF WHOLE
大惊小怪	Big surprise small surprise	Big deal out of nothing
生离死别	Live apart die farewell	Life and death trauma
同甘共苦	Same sweet share bitter	Through thick and thin

–   pairs of directional morphemes and synonyms interwoven

EXAMPLES	MEANINGS OF MORPHEMES	MEANING OF WHOLE
南腔北调	South accent north tone	Speak with mixed accent
东奔西跑	East run west run	Running around
东张西望	East look west look	Looking around

– pairs of directional morphemes and antonyms interwoven

EXAMPLE	MEANINGS OF MORPHEMES	MEANING OF WHOLE
南来北往	South come north go	To and fro

– pairs of numbers and synonyms interwoven

EXAMPLES	MEANINGS OF MORPHEMES	MEANING OF WHOLE
一干二净	1 dry 2 clean	Completely gone
四平八稳	4 level 8 stable	Even and steady
五颜六色	5 color 6 color	Colorful
乱七八糟	Chaos 7 8 mess	Total mess

– pairs of numbers and antonyms interwoven

EXAMPLES	MEANINGS OF MORPHEMES	MEANING OF WHOLE
七上八下	7 up 8 down	Very nervous
一暴十寒	1 sunned 10 cold	No perseverance

三长两短	3 long 2 short	Unforeseen death/illness
九死一生	9 die 1 live	Difficult survival

- reduplication interwoven with synonyms

EXAMPLES	MEANINGS OF MORPHEMES	MEANING OF WHOLE
全心全意	Whole heart whole intent	Whole-heartedly
称王称霸	Claim king claim ruler	Be pretender to the throne
大拆大卸	Big take apart big dismantle	Tear apart in a big way

- reduplication interwoven with antonyms

EXAMPLES	MEANINGS OF MORPHEMES	MEANING OF WHOLE
自生自灭	Self live self perish	Fending for oneself
不破不立	Not break not establish	Destroy old to build new
何去何从	Where go where come	Make your decision!

- reduplication interwoven with numbers

EXAMPLE	MEANINGS OF MORPHEMES	MEANING OF WHOLE
不三不四	Not 3 not 4	Of questionable character

While some of the disyllabic pairs can be freely occurring words, e.g., the underlined syllables in 一干二净、全心全意、南腔北调, none of the contiguous disyllables that result from interweaving can be freely occurring words.

2.3.4 Other Morphological Processes in Chinese

Compounding is not the only kind of morphological process in Chinese. The other two kinds are affixation and reduplication.

Affixation. Words can be formed by adding affixes to the root. Depending on whether an affix is attached to the beginning or the end of the root, we will call the affix either *prefix* or *suffix*.

- Prefixes:
  - 第 *dì*: 第一, 第二, 第三 (first, second, third, respectively)
  - 老 *lǎo*: 老虎 (tiger), 老鹰 (eagle), 老婆 (wife), and 老公 (husband)
- Suffixes:
  - Noun endings:
    - 子 -*zi*: 儿子 (son), 桌子 (table), 房子 (house), 扇子 (fan)
    - 头 -*tou*: 里头/外头/前头/后头 (inside/outside/front/back)
    - 儿 -*r*: 花儿 (flower), 画儿 (painting)
    - 们 -*men*: 我们/你们/他们 (wo/you (pl.)/they)
    - 学 -*xué*: 物理学 (physics), 化学 (chemistry), 文学 (literature)
    - 性 -*xìng*: 稳定性 (stability), 可靠性 (reliability)
  - Verb endings: aspectual particles:
    - 了 -*le* (咗 in Cantonese): 我吃了一碗饭。 (I ate a bowl of food.)
    - 着 -*zhe* (*gen* in Cantonese): 我吃着饭呢。 (I am eating.)
    - 过 -*guo*: 我吃过中国饭。 (I have eaten Chinese food.)

Reduplication. Either monosyllabic or disyllabic root morphemes can be reduplicated. In the case of disyllabic forms such as AB, there are two patterns, ABAB or AABB, depending on the syntactic categories of the elements being reduplicated. The third example in each of the following two groups is a nice illustration of the syntactic role of reduplication. Reduplication is not found in English and other European languages.

- Verbal:
  - 看→看看 (look→take a look)
  - 商量→商量商量 (discuss→have a discussion, ABAB)
  - 高兴→高兴高兴 (to be happy→have some fun, ABAB)
- Adjectival:
  - 红→红红 (red→reddish)
  - 漂亮→漂漂亮亮 (pretty→very pretty, AABB)
  - 高兴→高高兴兴 (happy→very happy, AABB)

- Nominal:
  - 人→人人 (person→every person)
  - 个→个个 [(some) measure of (entity)→each and every (entity)]

It is worth pointing out that along with the additional meaning of each/every, reduplication may also change the syntactic function. In the second example, the measure word 个 can be used as a nominal expression by itself when reduplicated, e.g., as a subject in a sentence.

2.3.5　Ionization (离合)

A morphosyntactic phenomenon that poses a challenge to NLP in Chinese is "ionization," i.e., the process by which component morphemes of words are separated from each other, such as by inserted materials between the morphemes or movement of one of the morphemes away from its mate. For example, 理发 (cut-hair) is a word on grounds of syntactic distribution and independence of meaning. But it is possible to say 理短发 (have short haircut), 理一个发 (have a haircut), or 发理了吗 (hair has been cut?), etc.

2.4　WORD IDENTIFICATION AND SEGMENTATION

The distinctness of words from the written unit of characters, coupled with the writing convention that leaves no space between characters and words, creates a difficult problem for word identification in Chinese. It makes *segmentation* a necessary requirement for Chinese NLP. From the perspective of the whole sentence, segmentation is cutting character strings into word-size chunks; but from the perspective of the characters, word segmentation in effect requires combining character strings into word chunks.

2.5　SUMMARY

As necessary preparation for morphological processing later in the book, this chapter describes the morphological units of words and morphemes in Chinese, their distinctness from the units of the written script, as well as the major word formation processes in Chinese.

·　·　·　·　·

CHAPTER 3

Challenges in Chinese Morphological Processing

3.1 INTRODUCTION

This chapter enumerates the various characteristics of Chinese and the Chinese text that create special challenges to morphological processing. Some of the characteristics have to do with Chinese characters, such as their large number, the existence of simplified, traditional, nonstandard, and dialectal variants, the existence of multiple character coding standards, not to mention the existence of homographs, which represent different sounds and meanings with the same graph; some are purely textual, having to do with orthographic, printing and punctuation conventions; some are linguistic, for instance, the paucity of grammatical markers and extensive ambiguity, out-of-vocabulary (OOV) words such as names, transliterations, acronyms and abbreviations, and regional and stylistic variation.

3.2 CHINESE CHARACTERS

3.2.1 Large Number of Characters

An immediate difference from an alphabetic system is the much larger number of characters as compared with the number of letters, even though the exact number of existent Chinese characters cannot be precisely ascertained. The number of Chinese characters contained in the well-known 康熙字典 (Kangxi dictionary) published in 1716 is approximately 47,035 [Kangxi 1716], although a large number of these are rarely used variant forms accumulated throughout history. Published in 1994, the 中华字海 (Zhonghua Zihai dictionary) contains 87,019 Chinese characters [Zhonghua 1994]. The actual number of characters for practical use, however, is much smaller. Full literacy in the Chinese language requires knowledge of only between 3,000 and 4,000 characters, of which 1,000 characters may cover 92% written materials, and 3,000 characters cover more than 99%. Due to the large number of characters, much more than the alphanumeric set, for computer processing purpose, Chinese characters are encoded in 16+ bits.

3.2.2   Simplified and Traditional Characters

One needs to be aware that there are two sets of characters in use, namely, traditional characters 繁体 and simplified characters 简体. Simplified characters are officially used in the People's Republic of China (PRC, mainland), Singapore, Malaysia, and the United Nations. Taiwan, Hong Kong, and Macau use traditional characters. Overseas Chinese communities generally use traditional characters, but simplified characters are used among mainland Chinese immigrants. Simplified characters are mostly distinguished by having fewer strokes, with simplified components.

Important to bear in mind when converting between the two kinds of characters is the fact that some distinctions in traditional characters are conflated in simplified characters. For example, 乾 and 幹 are distinct in traditional characters, representing "dry" and "to do" respectively, but both meanings are represented by the simplified 干; 遊 and 游 represent "travel" and "swim" respectively, but they are conflated into 游 in the simplified form. Therefore, there is no one-to-one correspondence between the traditional and simplified character sets, making the conversion between the two styles less than straightforward. Conversion from simplified to traditional is typically more problematic, as one and the same character may have to be converted to different characters, as the example with 干 above illustrates.

3.2.3   Variant Characters

Complicating the processing of Chinese texts further, in addition to simplified and traditional characters, there are also characters that have the same meanings and sounds but different shapes, called variant characters 异体字. Most of the characters in the Kangxi dictionary are variant characters, which have fallen into general disuse. Variant characters often share the same components as their standard counterparts, for example, 裏 and 裡, 膀 and 髈, 杯 and 盃, 秘 and 祕, 毙 and 斃. Interestingly, in mainland China, 够 is the variant of 够, while it is the opposite in Taiwan. Although not officially accepted, the use of variants characters, regarded as a sign of individuality, has had a recent surge among young Internet users in informal settings.

3.2.4   Dialect Characters and Dialectal Use of Standard Characters

Although written Chinese shares a substantial core of vocabulary and grammar among speakers of different dialects, one needs to be aware of the existence of dialectal characters 方言字, which can cause problems for text processing. Some of the major dialects, such as Cantonese, Shanghai, and southern Min, have created characters that are only comprehensible to speakers of these dialects. At the same time, these dialects have also borrowed characters liberally from the standard character set and put them to new uses incomprehensible to speakers of other dialects. The need for dialectal characters and the dialectal use of standard characters is dictated by the existence of dialect-specific words absent from the common core vocabulary shared by all dialects. Although dialectal characters and dialectal use of standard characters do not enjoy high prestige, they can often be found in popular publications. The following are some examples from Cantonese:

CANTONESE	MEANING	MEANINGS OF CHARACTERS	MANDARIN
而家	Now	But–home	现在
同埋	And	Same–bury	和
边个	Who	Side–measure	哪位
边道	Where	Side–path	哪儿
听日	Tomorrow	Listen–day	明天
头先	Just now	Head–first	刚才
呢的	These	Particle–particle	这些
古仔	Story	Ancient–son	故事
点解	Why	Point–resolve	为什么
俾	Give	Slave	给
郁	Move	Lush	动
企	Stand	Enterprise	站
仲	Still	Mid	还
紧	-ing	Tight	着

It can be seen that most dialectal uses of standard characters are based on the principle of phonetic loan, namely, a character is borrowed for its approximate sound and the original meaning of the character is ignored. Some examples from Shanghai and Southern Min are given below:

SHANGHAI	MANDARIN	ENGLISH
侬	你	You
伊	她/他	He/she
接棍	利害	Tough
交归	非常	Very
伐	不	Not
白相	玩	Play

SOUTHERN MIN	MANDARIN	ENGLISH
阮	我(们)	I/we
暗	晚	Late
郎	人	Person
呷	吃	Eat
叨位	哪儿	Where
的括	得意	Complacent

In addition to borrowing from standard characters, dialects have also created their own characters. While a few are based on meanings, such as the Cantonese 冇 for "not have" (derived from the standard character 有 "to have"), most are phonetically based. For example, in Cantonese, most created characters have the mouth radical 口, explicitly indicating that the character is used for its sound alone and the original meaning is irrelevant: 吡、喎、㗎、啫、哟、咁、噉、嘢、吓、唔、嘅、咁、咗、嚟、喈、喇、嘟.

3.2.5   Multiple Character Encoding Standards

Chinese documents and web pages also use different encoding standards, reflecting the differences in time and location of their creation. There are mainly three different standards, namely, GB, Big5, and Unicode. The GB encoding scheme is most often used for simplified characters, while Big5 for traditional characters. Unicode can be used to encode both.

GB/GBK. Guóbiāo (国标), GB for short, is the abbreviation for "National Standard" in Chinese. The GB encoding scheme is the standard used in China mainland, Singapore, and Malaysia. The GB character set represents 7,445 characters. It includes 6,763 simplified characters. The initial version of GB, known as GB2312-80, contained only one code point for each character. If a character is from GB2312-80, the MSB, i.e., bit-8 of each byte, is set to 1 and therefore becomes an 8-bit character. Otherwise, the byte is interpreted as American Standard Code for Information Interchange (ASCII). Every Chinese character is represented by a 2-byte code. The most significant bit (MSB) of both the first and second bytes are set. Thus, they can be easily identified from documents that contain both GB characters and regular ASCII characters.

The problem of the GB encoding scheme is its inability to cover traditional Chinese characters. Hence, the China government developed the GBK scheme, which is short for 国标扩展 Guóbiāo Kuòzhǎn (Extension of National Standard) and is an extension of GB2312. The "extended" GB character set includes 14,240 traditional characters and the scheme is used by Simplified Microsoft

Windows 95 and 98. Released by the China Standard Press on March 17, 2000, and updated on November 20, 2000, GB18030 supersedes all previous versions of GB. As of August 1, 2006, support for this character set is officially mandatory for all software products sold in the PRC. It supports both simplified and traditional Chinese characters.

BIG5. Big5 is the character encoding standard, with 13,000 characters, most commonly for traditional Chinese characters, used by Taiwan, Hong Kong, and Macau. Every Chinese character is represented by a 2-byte code. The first byte ranges from $0 \times \bar{A}$ to $0 \times F9$, while the second byte ranges from 0×40 to $0 \times 7E$, $0 \times \bar{A}$ to $0 \times FE$. Note that the MSB of the 2-byte code is always set. Thus, in a document that contains both traditional Chinese characters and regular ASCII characters, the ASCII characters are still represented with a single byte. Big5 can also be used with ASCII. The MSB of ASCII characters is always 0. The MSB of the first byte of a Big5 character is always 1; this distinguishes it from an ASCII character. The second byte has 8 significant bits. Therefore, Big5 is an 8-bit encoding with a 15-bit code space.

Unicode. Unicode is an industry standard that allows computers to consistently represent and manipulate text expressed in most of the world's writing systems. Developed in tandem with the universal character set (UCS) standard and published as the Unicode standard, Unicode consists of a repertoire of more than 100,000 characters. The Unicode coding scheme originates from East Asia. Different countries in this area originally had different character encoding schemes based on the ASCII scheme. The usual approach is to use 2 bytes to code 1 character. This creates great difficulty. That is, the code needs to detect whether one code represents 1 character or half a character. If the latter, it has to be further determined whether the character is the first half or second half. Eventually, the Unicode scheme was invented to make use of 2-byte codes to represent any characters.

Unicode can be implemented by different character encodings. The most commonly used encodings are the Unicode transformation format (UTF)-8 (which uses 1 byte for all ASCII characters, which have the same code values as in the standard ASCII encoding, and up to 4 bytes for other characters), the now-obsolete UCS-2 (which uses 2 bytes for all characters, but does not include every character in the Unicode standard), and UTF-16 (which extends UCS-2, using 4 bytes to encode characters missing from UCS-2). The Unicode scheme is capable of representing characters in any languages including Chinese. Unicode deals with the issue of simplified and traditional characters as part of the project of Han unification by including code points for each. This was rendered necessary by the fact that the correspondence between simplified characters and traditional characters is not one-to-one. While this means that the Unicode system can display both simplified and traditional characters, it also means that different localization files are needed for each type. The characters in Unicode are a superset of the characters in GB and Big5, thus it is easy to convert directly from GB or Big5 into Unicode.

3.3   TEXTUAL CONVENTIONS

3.3.1   Printing Format

Variable orientation. Lines of text in Chinese can be printed either from left to right 中国是一个大国 (China is a big country) or right to left 国大个一是国中, horizontally or vertically, as is done in older books.

No space between words. A salient characteristic that has important consequences for computer processing is that Chinese texts are written and printed without any white space between words, which can be used in alphabetically written languages to identify word boundaries. A necessary first step in Chinese text processing is therefore the segmentation of text, i.e., cutting the strings of contiguous characters into segments of words.

No upper/lower-case distinction. Another distinctive property of Chinese characters that poses additional challenge for Chinese language processing is the absence of the distinction between upper and lower cases, which is used by some languages to mark grammatical functions. For example, proper nouns in English and all nouns in German are started with capital letters. Although proper nouns, including personal names and place names, used to be underlined in Chinese texts, it is no longer a prevalent practice. Hence, the identification of proper nouns poses a particular challenge in processing Chinese text. A related consequence is that acronyms and abbreviations, which are often capitalized in alphabetic writing, cannot be easily identified in Chinese.

No distinction between native and transliterated words. Unlike Japanese which uses *kata kana* symbols to exclusively spell words of foreign origin, transliterated words in Chinese are not visually distinct from native words.

No hyphenation. In some languages, hyphens are used to indicate morpheme boundaries when a line of text needs to be broken up. No hyphens are used in Chinese texts. This is because with the exception of foreign loanwords, characters are largely co-terminus with morphemes, thus obviating the need for hyphens.

Separator in foreign names. A dot "·" is used to separate the first and last names in transliterated names, including those of foreign persons and non-Han minority groups. An English name 理查德·米尔豪斯·尼克松 (Richard Milhous Nixon) and an Uygur name 玉素甫·卡迪尔汗 (Yusuf Qadr Khan) are but two such examples. While the presence of the dot can be used as a heuristic in NLP, most often the full name is not used and hence no dot is used.

No separator comma in large numbers. Unlike English, the separator comma to mark every 1,000 is not consistently used. Thus, the number 300,000 can be written simply as 300000.

Date and address format. In Chinese, both date and address formats follow the "large to small" principle, namely, the larger units preceding the smaller ones. Thus, June 3, 2009, is written as 二零零九年六月三日 (2009, June 3rd), and #35 Heping Lane, Chaoyang District, Beijing, China, is rendered as 中国北京朝阳区和平里35号 (China, Beijing, Chaoyang District, Heping Lane, #35).

Percentage. Instead of N%, Chinese uses the format of %N. Thus, 30% is represented as 百分之三十 (percent 30). There are some informal variants used, for example, in Malaysia that follow the English format, such as 三十巴仙 (30 bāxiān), where the percent part is also transliterated from English.

Currency. Unlike English, where the cent is the only other basic unit in addition to the dollar, the dime is also a basic unit along with cent and dollar. Thus, 50 cents is rendered as 5 dimes 五毛/五角.

3.3.2 Punctuation Practice

Although modern Chinese text has adopted the regular use of punctuation marks (with the exceptions of some classified ads and telegraphic messages), punctuation practice in Chinese is quite different from that in English. Especially noteworthy is the greater use of commas, which are used not only to terminate phrases and clauses but also to frequently mark syntactic units analogous to English sentences. Very often, a period mark only occurs at the end of a paragraph.

Book titles are enclosed in double-angled brackets, as in 《大学》. Also, the pause mark "、" that is unique to Chinese is used to separate items on a list (e.g., 手、脚、腿…等, which means hand, foot, leg . . . etc.).

3.4   LINGUISTIC CHARACTERISTICS

3.4.1 Few Formal Morphological Markers

Compared with English and other European languages, words in Chinese have few formal morphological marker. Verbs have no marker for grammatical categories such as tense, person, and number. Nouns have no markers of number, gender, and case.

1. No verbal inflections

    (a) No tense

    Chinese has no tense. Therefore, a verb will have the same form for all the different time references. In the following examples, the words in **bold** in English are different in form but they all correspond to the same 是 in Chinese:
    – 我过去 是 学生。 (I **was** a student.)
    – 我现在 是 学生。 (I **am** a student.)
    – 我将来 是 学生。 (I **will be** a student.)

    (b) No personal and number agreements

    In English, a verb may take on different inflectional endings depending on the person and the number of the subject. For example, for third person singular subject pronouns *he*, *she*, and *it*, the verb has to have an *-s* ending. Chinese, however, has no such agreement at all:

– 我 去。(I **go**.)
– 她 去。(She **goes**.)

2. No nominal endings

(a) No number marking

Chinese does not have the singular and plural distinction for nouns, as shown in the following:

– 我的书 My book(s)

(b) No gender marking

Chinese does not have the gender distinction of masculinity and femininity, unlike Spanish, which has grammatical gender for nouns, both human and inanimate, as can be seen by the different articles required, i.e., *el* for masculine and *la* for feminine.

MASCULINE	FEMININE
El chico (boy)	La chica (girl)
El jardin (garden)	La universidad (university)
El libro (book)	La revista (magazine)
El miedo (fear)	La libertad (liberty)

(c) No case marking

Chinese does not have case ending for nouns either, unlike English, which still distinguishes the subject and object cases for pronouns. In the following pairs of sentences, the English pronouns in **bold** are in different cases. But no such distinction exists in Chinese:

– **I** love **her**. vs. **She** loves **me**. (I=subject case; me=object case; she=subject case; her=object case)
– 我爱她她爱我。(我=both subject and object case; 她=both subject and object case)

Due to the paucity of morphological markings in Chinese, greater use will have to be made of semantic information in the morphological processing of Chinese.

3.4.2 Parts of Speech

One of the most basic grammatical concepts is parts of speech (POS). In many languages, parts of speech are explicitly marked. Thus, nouns may be marked for number, gender, and case, and verbs are inflected for tense, number, person, etc. In these languages, telling the POS of a word is relatively straightforward. POS exists in Chinese as well, although they are often not explicitly marked.

Few POS clues. Although sometimes POS in Chinese can be inferred from the kind of component morphemes in words, such as 子, 性, 度 for nouns, most of the time POS have to be inferred from the grammatical contexts. This can be illustrated by the word for *help* in Chinese. The word *help* in English can be either a noun as in "thank you for your help" or a verb as in "please help me." The word can be translated by three words in Chinese all containing the morpheme 帮, i.e., 帮, 帮助, and帮忙. The three, however, are not interchangeable, as is clear from the following examples:

1. "Thank you for your help" can only be rendered as:
   – 谢谢你的帮助(*帮, *帮忙).
2. "Please help me" can be translated in two ways:
   – 请你帮助/帮(*帮忙)我.
3. "I would like to ask you to help" can be translated only as:
   – 我想请你帮忙(*帮助, *帮).

In the first sentence, since only 帮助 can be used after 你的 (your), it seems that 帮助 is a noun. Neither 帮 nor 帮忙 can be used in this context. In the second sentence, since 帮助 occurs after the subject 你 (you), it appears that it can be a verb as well, just like the English word *help*. 帮 can also be used here and hence is also a verb. But 帮忙, although a verb, does not seem to be the right kind in this context. In the third sentence, even though a verb is called for after 你, both 帮助 and 帮 (which we just said can be verbs) cannot be used here. Only 帮忙 can be used. A closer look reveals that the context for this sentence is different, in that there is no object after *help* here. Hence, the emerging pattern for the usage of the three words for "help" is as follows:

1. 帮助 is both a noun and a verb that takes an object (a transitive verb).
2. 帮 can only be a verb that takes an object (a transitive verb).
3. 帮忙 can only be a verb that does not take an object (an intransitive verb).

From the case of *help*, we can see that POS in Chinese indeed exists. Even though words are not marked explicitly for POS, there are strict restrictions on whether they can appear in a particular grammatical context.

Multiple POS. In Chinese, the same words can have more than one part of speech. Some examples are given below:

1. Both noun and verb
   - 经济的发展很迅速。 (Economy development is very rapid.)
   - 经济发展得很迅速。 (The economy developed very rapidly.)

   The word 的 in the first sentence requires a noun to follow. Thus, 发展 (development) has to be a noun. On the other hand, the word 得 (pronounced the same as 的 above) in the second sentence requires a verb to precede it. Thus, 发展 (to develop) has to be a verb here.

2. Both verb and preposition
   - 他在家。(He is at home.)
   - 他在家吃饭。 (He eats food at home.)

   The word 在 (*zài*, i.e., to stay) has to be the verb in the first sentence, as every sentence should have a verb and neither 他 (he) nor 家 (home) can be a verb. But the main verb in the second sentence is 吃 (eat). Therefore, 在 cannot be the main verb. It has been treated variously as a preposition or a co-verb. Similarly in the following pair:
   - 我给了他很多钱。(I gave him a lot of money.)
   - 我给他买了一本书。(I bought a book for him.)

The word 给 (*gěi*, i.e., to give) has to be the verb in the first sentence, as every sentence should have a verb. However, since the main verb in the second sentence is 买 (to buy), the word 给 (*gěi*) cannot be a verb; in this case, it means "for" (i.e., 给他 means for him).

3.4.3 Homonyms and Homographs

Homophony refers to the phenomenon of the same sound representing more than one meaning. In English, for example, what is spelled as "saw" can mean at least two different things, i.e., a tool for carpenters or the past tense for the verb "to see." Interestingly, "see" also has two meanings, i.e., perception by the eye and the religious reference to the seat of power as in "the holy see." The given examples have identical spellings for the different meanings. But homophony is not restricted to such cases at all. "Meat" and "meet" are not spelled the same and have different meanings, but they have identical sounds. So they are also bona fide homophones.

Compared with English, Chinese has a much smaller number of possible syllables due to its simpler syllable structure, which does not allow consonant clusters, and only a limited number of final consonants. There are only some 400+ syllables in Mandarin without the tones or about 1,100 with tones. This is very different from English, which has over 80,000 possible syllables. Another difference is the largely monosyllabic nature of Chinese morphemes. These two facts taken together mean that there are fewer syllables for forming morphemes. Given the large number of meanings any language has to express, many morphemes then have to share the same syllables. Extensive homophony thus results. Take the example of the syllable *shi*. It has close to 30 distinct meanings: 市 (city), 事 (matter), 世 (generation), 式 (style), 室 (room), 视 (vision), 示 (show), 士 (official), 试 (try), 誓 (promise), 释 (explain), 饰 (decorate), 适 (suit), 侍 (wait on), 柿 (persimmon), 是 (be), 氏 (last name), 势 (power), 似 (resemble), 逝 (pass) , 仕 (official), 弑 (kill), 嗜 (like), 拭 (wipe).

The famous linguist Chao [1968] once illustrated this phenomenon rather dramatically with a mock classical style tale using one single-syllable *shi*, which begins, 石室詩士施氏，嗜獅，誓 食十獅 "Shi shi shi shi Shi shi, shi shi, shi shi shi shi," and translates as "Mr. Shi, a poet who lived in a stone house, liked to eat lions and promised to eat 10 lions." Those who have used Chinese word processors will get a good sense of the extent of homophony in Chinese. When you type in a syllable, you will be presented a list of characters (the length of the list depends on the number of homonyms available to that syllable) and you have to choose the desired character from that list.

One the other hand, *homographs* also exist in Chinese, i.e., the same character that has more than one sound and meaning. For example, the character 地 can be read either as *dì* or *de*, meaning ground and the adverbial marker, respectively; 着 is pronounced as *zhe* denoting the durative aspect, but it is pronounced as *zháo* in words such as 着急 (to worry) and着火 (catch fire).

For the purposes of text processing, the indeterminacy caused by homographs poses a more serious problem than homophony.

3.4.4 Ambiguity

A major challenge in NLP is ambiguity. There are different kinds of ambiguity, lexical as well as structural, resulting from differences in word meanings or structural configurations. In Chinese NLP, sources of ambiguity are often caused by special characteristics of Chinese writing. For example, the sentence 他很好吃 can mean either "he likes to eat" or the bizarre but possible "he is delicious to eat," depending on whether the character 好 is interpreted as an adjective, i.e., good, or a verb, i.e., to like. This is a case of lexical ambiguity due to 好 being a homograph. The process to resolve such *lexical ambiguity* is commonly referred to as word sense disambiguation (WSD).

Structural ambiguity results from having more than one way to analyze a complex linguistic unit. Due to the need to segment character strings into words in Chinese, the possibility of multiple segmentation arises. At the most basic level, a character string can exhibit overlapping ambiguity, combinatorial ambiguity, or a mixture of both.

Overlapping (crossing) ambiguity 交集型歧义. Out of the string ABC, if AB and BC are both possible words, then ABC exhibits overlapping ambiguity. For example, 网球场 (tennis court) can be segmented as either 网球+场 or 网+球场. 美国会 can be segmented as either 美国+会 (America will) or 美+ 国会 (US congress).

Combinatorial ambiguity 组合型歧义. Out of the string AB, if A, B, and AB are all possible words, then AB exhibits combinatorial ambiguity. For example, 才能 can be segmented as a noun 才能/n, meaning talent, or 才/d能/v as the combination of the adverb 才 (only then) and modal verb 能 (able to). Other examples include 学会, which can be segmented as either 学会/n (society) or 学/v会/v (learn how to), 学生会 as either 学生会/n (student society) or 学生/n会/v (students will), 马上 as either 马/n上/p (back of a horse) or 马上/adv. (immediately), 个人 as either 个/m人/n (one person) or 个人/n (individual), etc.

Mixed type 混合型歧义. In the string ABC, if AB and BC, and A or B or C are possible words, then ABC exhibits a mixed type, including both overlapping and combinatorial ambiguity. For examples, out of the string 太平淡 (too dull), 太平 (peaceful), 平淡 (dull), 太 (over), 平 (flat), 淡 (plain) are all possible words, and out of the string 人才能, 人才 (talent), 才能 (enabled), 人 (person), 才 (thus), and 能 (able) are all possible words.

Ambiguity can also be categorized according to at what level and with what kind of contextual clues it can be resolved.

Pseudo (local) ambiguity. Despite the multiple segmentation possibilities, there is really only one way to segment the strings in question, in reality. For example, in both of the following pairs of sentences, it is clear how the underlined strings should be segmented:

1. (a) 他将来北京工作。将/来/=will come: He will come to Beijing to work.
    (b) 将来北京一定会更繁荣。将来/adv.=future: Beijing will become more prosperous in the future.
2. (a) 从马上摔下来。马/上/=up the horse: Fall down from the horse.
    (b) 我马上就来。马上/=immediately: I will come immediately.

True (global) ambiguity. The ambiguity found in the following two sentences is *true* in the sense that the underlined strings can be segmented in more than one way in real usage. The resolution of such ambiguity can only rely on access to more global type of contextual clues such as the topic.

–   这种技术应用于国防领域。应/用于 or 应用/于 ("This kind of technology should be used in the field of defense." or "This kind of technology is used in the field of defense.")
–   该研究所得到的奖金很多。研究/所 or 研究所 ("This research got a lot of fund." or "This research institute got a lot of fund.")

As the processed unit becomes bigger, the potential for ambiguity resolution is enhanced, thanks to the access to greater amount of contextual information in longer discourses. For example, the meaning of a character can vary between a number of different senses, but in a sentential context, only one sense "makes sense." Sometimes, ambiguity remains even in a sentential context while a paragraph contains enough information to resolve the ambiguity.

3.4.5   OOV Words 未登录词

Another major challenge for NLP in Chinese is how to deal with new words not found in existing dictionaries. They include acronyms and abbreviations, names of people, places, organizations, and transliteration of foreign words.

Acronyms and abbreviations. Abbreviations are legion in Chinese and new ones are created all the time. Even though some established ones, such as 北约 (NATO), may have found their ways into dictionaries, most will not. The ways to abbreviate also look fairly idiosyncratic. For example, in mainland China, 北京大学 (Beijing University) becomes 北大 (Beida), but 清华大学 (Tsinghua University) becomes 清华 (Tsinghua) and not 清大.[1] For another example, 中央银行 (Central Bank) is abbreviated as 央行 and not 中行. Abbreviations can also exhibit ambiguity, e.g., 中大 can refer to either 中山大学 (Zhongshan University in China) or 中文大学 (The Chinese University of Hong Kong).

Chinese names. Another kind of OOV words are personal names. Since names cannot be exhaustively listed in dictionaries, it is necessary to know the rules of formation, so that algorithms can be devised to parse them effectively.

Chinese surnames are either one- or two-syllable long, with monosyllabic surnames constituting the majority. Examples of disyllabic surnames are 欧阳、上官、端木, etc. Although there are a few hundred surnames, the top five 王, 陈, 李, 张, 刘 constitute over one-third of all surnames and the first 100 or so cover about 90%.

Given names can also be one- or two-syllable long, with disyllabic given names being in the majority. Although the set of characters used in given names is much larger than that used for surnames, there are some high-frequency characters, such as 英, 华, 玉, 秀, 明, 珍, which cover 10.35% of the 3,345 character pool and the most frequent 410 cover up to 90%. The gender of the bearer of given names often can be deduced from the characters used. Typical characters used in female names include 花, 秀, 娟, 媛, etc.

Full names in Chinese are therefore two- to four-syllable long, with most having three syllables. However, married women in Taiwan, Hong Kong, and overseas Chinese communities have adopted the western tradition of taking the surnames of their husbands. But unlike their western counterparts, they also retain their maiden names, which are placed after their husbands' surname. Therefore, their full names follow the pattern of: husband's surname+maiden surname+given name, most often being four-syllable long.

Transliterations. Transliterations are approximations in sound of foreign words using native phonetic resources. In Chinese, characters are borrowed to transliterate similar sounding foreign

---

[1]Note that 清大 for 清华大学 is acceptable in Taiwan.

words. These characters are used for their sounds only, without regard to what they originally mean. In practice, characters that are often used to transliterate foreign words tend to be vague in meaning. Some examples are 斯, 司, 尔, 尼, 克, 伊, 拉, 朗, 顿, etc. Some transliterated place and personal names are伊拉克 (Iraq), 伊朗 (Iran), 克拉克 (Clark), and 克林顿 (Clinton). On the other hand, sometimes semantic as well as phonetic considerations enter into the creation of transliterated terms. For example, blogger is rendered as 博客 *bókè*, which is not really very close phonetically to the original word but is chosen for its meaning (博客, i.e., many guests).

Despite the tendency to prefer meaning translations in Chinese such as 蜜月 (honeymoon), transliterations are necessary because personal and place names often do not have transparent meanings. With the exception of long-established loanwords such as 马达 (motor) and 引擎 (engine), most transliterations of foreign words such as place names and personal names fall into the category of OOV words.

3.4.6 Regional Variation

Despite outward appearances, Chinese is, in fact, a family of languages including Mandarin, Cantonese, Shanghai, Min, Hakka, etc. These languages, popularly known as *dialects*, are often mutually unintelligible when spoken mainly due to great differences in pronunciation. They do, however, share the same writing system, which makes communication between the dialect speakers possible.

Although written Chinese (which is the main concern of the present volume) does share greater similarity than the spoken varieties, differences do exist in vocabulary and grammar between the dialects.

3.4.7 Stylistic Variation

The mixing of styles is frequently observed in written Chinese. Many classical style expressions can be found in modern writing. This can pose a problem for word segmentation. As observed earlier, many formerly free morphemes, such as 饮 (drink) and 食 (eat) in classical Chinese, have become bound in modern Chinese. With the mixing of styles in the same text, then it may be hard to have a uniform standard for segmentation.

3.5 SUMMARY

This chapter outlines the various linguistic and textual characteristics of Chinese, which pose special challenges in NLP. These characteristics range from extensive variation (regional, stylistic, in characters and their encoding) to special textual conventions of printing and punctuation, and from the great amount of ambiguity and the lack of explicit grammatical marking to the many OOV words such as names, abbreviations, and transliterations. All of these characteristics lead to difficulty in word identification and segmentation, which will be addressed in the next chapter.

CHAPTER 4

Chinese Word Segmentation

4.1 INTRODUCTION

It is generally agreed among researchers that word segmentation is a necessary first step in Chinese language processing. Unlike English text in which words are delimited by white spaces, in Chinese text, sentences are represented as strings of Chinese characters (*hanzi*) without similar natural delimiters between them. Here is an English sentence "I am a student," which is expressed in Chinese as "我是一个学生." In the English sentences, there is a white space between the words, so the computer can easily identify "student" as a word by the indicator of the white space. On the contrary, in Chinese, there are no delimiters that explicitly indicate the boundaries between words, and it is necessary for the computer to combine the two characters "学" and "生" into a word. Therefore, the task of word segmentation is to identify the sequence of words and mark the boundaries in appropriate places from the sentence which is composed of a string of Chinese characters. The segmentation result of the sentence "我是一个学生" is "我/是/一个/学生." The formal definition of the word segmentation is as follows [Wu and Tseng 1993]:

Definition 1: A sentence S is a sequence of Chinese characters $(C_1, C_2, \ldots, C_M)$. An n-character token, namely word, of S beginning at the i-th character is an ordered n-tuple ""of the form, $(C_i, C_{i+1}, \ldots, C_{i+n-1})$. A partition W of a sentence partitions all its characters into non-overlapping tokens of various length $(C_1, C_2, \ldots, C_{i_1-1}), (C_{1_1}, C_{i_1+1}, \ldots, C_{i_2-1}), (C_{i_{N-1}}, C_{i_{N-1}+1}, \ldots, C_M)$. Name the elements of W as $(W_1, W_2, \ldots, W_N)$ respectively.

4.2 TWO MAIN CHALLENGES

Although the objective of Chinese word segmentation is clear, there are two main obstacles impeding the progress of Chinese word segmentation, namely, ambiguity (Chapter 3.4.4) and unknown word [also referred to as OOV words (Chapter 3.4.5)].

The ambiguity in Chinese word segmentation is a very serious problem. The ambiguity is generated in several ways. For one thing, most *hanzi* can occur in different positions within different words, and the lack of unambiguous word boundary indicators aggravates the situation. Example 4.2.1 shows how the Chinese character "产" (produce) can occur in four different positions. This state of affairs makes it impossible to simply list mutually exclusive subsets of *hanzi* that have distinct distributions, even though the number of *hanzi* in the Chinese writing system is in fact finite. As long as a *hanzi* can occur in different word internal positions, it cannot be relied upon to determine word boundaries.

Example 4.2.1: A *hanzi* can occur in multiple word internal positions.

POSITION	EXAMPLE
Left	产生 (to come up with)
Word by itself	产小麦 (to grow wheat)
Middle	生产线 (assembly line)
Right	生产 (to produce)

Ambiguity also arises because some *hanzi* are word components in certain contexts and words by themselves in other situations. As shown in Example 4.2.2, 鱼 (fish) can be considered as a word component in 章鱼 (octopus) only. It can also be a word by itself.

Example 4.2.2: Ambiguity in Chinese word segmentation.

(A) SEGMENTATION I				(B) SEGMENTATION II				
日文	章鱼	怎么	说?	日	文章	鱼	怎么	说?
Japanese	octopus	How	Say	Japan	article	fish	how	say

Presented with the string 章鱼 (octopus) in a Chinese sentence, a human or automatic segmenter would have to decide whether 鱼 (fish) should be a word by itself or form another word with the previous *hanzi*. Given that 日 (Japan), 文章 (article), 章鱼 (octopus), and 鱼 (fish) are all possible words in Chinese, how does one decide that "日鱼" is not? Obviously, it is not enough to know just what words are in the dictionary. In this specific case, a human segmenter can resort to world knowledge to resolve this ambiguity, knowing that the segmentation of "日 (Japan) 文章 (article) 鱼 (fish)" would not make any kind of real-world sense.

Besides, many *hanzi* have more than one pronunciation, which is another important reason of ambiguity. A *hanzi* with different pronunciations may be in different words or phrase combinations. The correct pronunciation depends upon word affiliation. For instance, "的" is pronounced *de0* when it is a pronominal modification marker, but *di4* in the word 目的 *mu4-di4* (goal).

In addition to the ambiguity problem, another problem that is often cited in the literature is the problem of OOV or unknown words. The unknown word problem arises because machine-readable dictionaries cannot possibly exhaustively list all the words encountered in NLP tasks. For one thing, although the number of *hanzi* generally remains constant, Chinese has several productive new word creation mechanisms, shown in Example 4.2.3. First of all, new words can be created through compounding, by which new words are formed by the combination of existing words, or through temporary means, by which components of existing words are extracted and combined to form new words. Second, new names are created by combining existing characters in a stochastic manner. Third, there are also transliterations of foreign names. Besides, numeric type compounding is another very important source. These are just a few of the many ways new words can be introduced in Chinese.

Example 4.2.3: Mechanisms of new words creation in Chinese

NEW WORDS CREATION MECHANISM	EXAMPLES
Word compounding	电脑 桌 (computer desk), 泥沙 (sofa)
Character combining	微软 (Microsoft), 非典 (SARS)
Foreign names	奥巴马 (Obahma), 加沙 (Gaza)
Numeric type compounding	二百港币 (two hundred HK dollars)

Therefore, the key to accurate word segmentation in Chinese is the successful resolution of these ambiguities and a proper way to handle OOV words. There are many approaches to Chinese word segmentation including dictionary-based, statistics-based, and learning-based approaches. The classification of the Chinese word segmentation approaches is shown in Figure 4.1. We will discuss how to solve the ambiguity and unknown word problems by going over each algorithm in the following section.

4.3   ALGORITHMS

The problem of Chinese word segmentation has been studied by researchers for many years. Several different algorithms have been proposed, which, generally speaking, can be classified into character-based approaches and word-based approaches. In this section, we will discuss each approach in detail and compare the performances among these approaches.

4.3.1   Character-Based Approach

The character-based approach is used to mainly process classical Chinese texts. Xue and Shen [2003] applied the maximum entropy (ME) model and achieved good results in the first bakeoff [Sproat and Emerson 2003]. According to the number of characters extracted, character-based approaches can be further divided into single character-based and multi-character-based approaches.

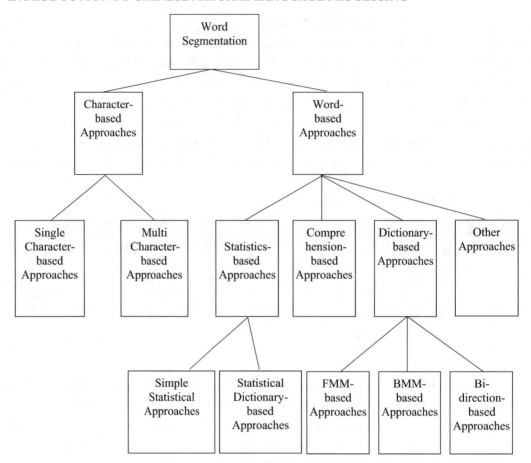

FIGURE 4.1: Classification of word segmentation approaches.

Single character–based approach. Single character-based approaches can be defined as purely mechanical processes that extract certain number of characters (to form a string) from texts. The single character-based approach is first used to process classical Chinese texts. It divides Chinese texts into single characters and is the simplest approach to segment Chinese text [Wu and Tian]. This method is used and enhanced later by Beijing Document Service to create the earlier version of Chinese Word Segmentation and Automated Indexing System (CWSAIS) [Chen and Zang 1999].

The majority of today's Chinese text processing systems generally do not employ the single character-based approach as the main segmentation approach, although some research groups have obtained encouraging results by only using this approach. The single-character-based approach is easy to implement. However, in general, its precision is low.

Multi-character-based approach. An estimation of the number of words in Modern Standard Chinese (MSC) according to the number of characters is: 5% one-character words, 75% two-character words, 14% three-character words, and 6% with four or more characters [Liu 1987]. That means that in the MSC, the majority of the words are bi-character, and many researchers turn their attention from focusing on single character to multi-characters.

The earlier multi-character-based approaches [Wu and Zhou 1984] segment texts into strings containing two (bigram), three, or more characters. Compared with the single-character approach, the multi-character approaches consistently yield better results. Since 75% of all commonly used Chinese word are made up of two characters, a popular approach is the bigram approach that segments a linear string of characters ABCDEF into AB, CD, EF and generates most of the correct Chinese word in a piece of text. A variation is the overlapping bigram that segments a sequence of Chinese characters ABCDEFG into AB BC CD DE EF FG. Similar results for using these two approaches have been reported. Another group [Deng et al.] implements another variant of the bigram approach by introducing a stop list to partially segment sentences before applying the bigram segmentation to create the index. In so doing, the size of the vocabulary is reduced significantly, but they find that the performance suffered no loss compared with the pure bigram approach.

H.T. Ng [1998] reformulated NLP as classification problems, in which the task is to observe some linguistic "context" $b \in B$ and predict the correct linguistic "class" $a \in A$. The procedure is to construct a classifier $\alpha : B \rightarrow A$, which, in turn, can be implemented with a conditional probability distribution p, such that $p(a|b)$ is the probability of "class" a given some "context" b. Ng used ME probability models to estimate the probability of a certain linguistic class occurring with a certain linguistic context.

Based on the ME model, Xue and Shen [2003] presented a novel algorithm. Instead of segmenting a sentence into word sequences directly, it first assigns position tags to each character. Later, based on these position tags, the characters are converted into word sequences. In a specific word, a character in the word will appear at a certain position. Given the assumption that we predefine the word as constructed by at most four characters, then the character will appear at the beginning, in the middle, at the end, or as a single-character word. Then, the sentences in Example 4.3.1 can be expressed as follows:

Example 4.3.1: (a) 上海计划到本世纪末实现人均国内生产总值五千美元。 (b) 上海/计划/到/本/世纪/末/实现/人均/国内/生产/总值/五千美元/。 (c) 上/B海/E计/B划/E到/S本/S世/B纪/E末/S实/B现/E人/B均/E国/B内/E生/B产/E总/B值/E五/B千/M美/M元/E。

where *B* stands for the first character of a multi-character word, *M* stands for intermediate character in a multi-character word (for words longer than two characters), *E* stands for the last character in a multi-character word, and *S* stands for one-character word.

The approach is implemented in two steps to process known words and unknown words, respectively. In the first step, it converts the output of the forward maximum matching (FMM) or backward maximum matching (BMM) [Teehan et al. 2000] into a character-wise form, where each character is assigned a position tag as described in Example 4.3.1 [Cheng et al. 1999; Sang and Veenstra 1999; Uchimoto et al. 2000]. These tags show possible character positions in words. For example, the character 本 is used as a single-character word in 一本书 (a book), at the end of a word in 剧本 (script), at the beginning of a word in 本来 (originally), or in the middle of a word in 基本上 (basically). In the second step, it uses the features to determine the tags of unknown words at location i using SVM [Vapnik 1995]. In other words, its feature set consists of the characters, the FMM and BMM outputs, and the previously tagged outputs. Based on these features and the output position tags, it can finally get the segmentation "迎/新春/联谊会/上" (welcome/new year/get-together party/at).

Recently, a few studies have applied conditional random fields (CRF) [Lafferty et al. 2001] to Chinese word segmentation [Peng et al. 2004; Tseng et al. 2005; Zhou et al. 2005] and have achieved competitive results.

CRF are undirected graphical models trained to maximize a conditional probability of the whole graph structure. A common case of a graph structure is a linear chain, which corresponds to a finite state machine, and is suitable for sequence labeling. A linear-chain CRF with parameters $\Lambda = \{\lambda_1, \ldots, \lambda_K\}$ defines a conditional probability for a label sequence $y = y_1 \ldots y_T$, given an input sequence $x = x_1 \ldots x_T$ to be:

$$P_\Lambda(y|x) = \frac{1}{Z_x} \exp \left[\sum_{t=1}^{T} \sum_{k} \lambda_k f_k(y_{t-1}, y_t, x) \right], \tag{4.1}$$

where Z_x is the normalization factor that makes the probability of all state sequences sum to 1, $f_k(y_{t-1}, y_t, x)$ is a feature function, and λ_k is a learned weight associated with feature f_k. The feature function measures any aspect of a state transition, $y_{t-1} \rightarrow y_t$, and the entire observation sequence, x. Large positive values for λ_k indicate a preference for an event, and large negative values make the event unlikely. The most probable label sequence for an input x, can be efficiently determined using the Viterbi algorithm.

$$y* = \underset{y}{\arg\max}\, P_\Lambda(y|x) \tag{4.2}$$

CRFs are trained using maximum likelihood estimation, i.e., maximizing the log-likelihood L_Λ of a given training set $T = \langle x_i, y_i \rangle_{i=1}^{N}$,

$$L_\Lambda = \sum_i \log P_\Lambda(y_i | x_i)$$

$$= \sum_i \left[\sum_{t=1}^{T} \sum_{k} \lambda_k f_k(y_{t-1}, y_t, x) - \log Z_{x_i} \right] \tag{4.3}$$

In this implementation, quasi-Newton method is used as the learning algorithm for parameter optimization, which has been shown to converge much faster. To avoid over-fitting, log-likelihood is penalized with Gaussian prior.

CRF is a discriminative model which can capture many correlated features of the inputs. Therefore, it is suitable in many tasks in NLP for sequence labeling. Since they are discriminatively trained, they are often more accurate than the generative models, even with the same features.

In applying character-based approaches, the most obvious advantage is simplicity and ease of application. This, in turn, leads to other advantages of reduced costs and minimal overheads in the indexing and querying process. As such, multi-character-based approaches, especially the ME and CRF approaches, have been found to be practical options that are implemented in many bench-marking standards.

4.3.2   Word-Based Approach

Word-based approaches, as the name implies, attempt to extract complete words from sentences. They can be further categorized as statistics-based, dictionary-based, comprehension-based, and learning-based approaches.

(a)   Dictionary-based approach

Among those word-based approaches, the most applicable, widely used are the two maximum matching methods, one scanning forward (FMM) and the other backward (BMM).

An FMM algorithm is a greedy search routine that walks through a sentence trying to find the longest string of *hanzi* starting from the very point in the sentence that matches a word entry in a predictionary. The first *i hanzi* are extracted from text. Only words with the same length in the dictionary would be searched and compared with the selected text. If no match is found, the last word of the selected text is cut and the process repeats until each word in the selected text has been found.

Example 4.3.2: (a) 关心食品销售情况。 (b) 关心食品和服装销售情况。

We take the Example 4.3.2(a) to illustrate the FMM algorithm. Assuming 关 (close), 心 (heart), and 关心 (care) are all listed in the dictionary, given a string of characters, the FMM algorithm always favors 关心 as a word, over 关-心 as a string of two words. This is because the segmenter first sets the character 关 as the very beginning of the character string and assumes the whole sentence as a long word. Then compare this word with the dictionary and search if there is a possible word which can be matched in the dictionary. If there is no such word in the dictionary, it will cut the last character, and the process is repeated till only one character is left. When it finds a word, for instance, 关心 (care), in the dictionary, it will stop searching and insert a word boundary marker rather than insert a word boundary marker between 关 and 心.

BMM method, which is optimized from the FMM algorithm, is similar to FMM except that it selects the latest i characters from the end of the text. Relatively, it was found to be more accurate. Example 4.3.2(b) can be segmented as "关心/食品/和服/装/销售/情况" and "关心/食品/和/服装/销售/情况" by FMM and BMM, respectively. However, a reverse dictionary, which is uncommon, is required by the BMM algorithm.

In addition, researchers combined FMM and BMM and proposed the bidirectional maximum matching approach. The algorithm first applies FMM and then BMM to improve accuracy. Also, it compares the two segmentation results to resolve any inconsistency and ambiguity. However, the dictionaries are doubled in size and the time taken for segmentation is at least twice longer than its individual counterparts.

(b)   Statistics-based approach

1.   Simple statistical approaches

As a representative of simple statistical approaches, Sproat and Shih [2000] relied on the mutual information of two adjacent characters to decide whether they form a two-character word. Given a string of characters $c_1, c_2 ... c_n$, the pair of adjacent characters with the largest mutual information greater than a predetermined threshold is grouped as a word. This process is repeated until there are no more pairs of adjacent characters with a mutual information value greater than the threshold. Mutual information between two characters x and y, denoted by $I(x, y)$, is calculated as in Equation (4.1):

$$I(x, y) = \frac{p(x, y)}{p(x)p(y)} \qquad (4.4)$$

where $p(x, y)$ denotes the probability that x and y occur adjacently in the corpus, and $p(x)$ and $p(y)$ denote the probabilities that x and y occur in the corpus, respectively.

Sun extended this approach by considering both mutual information and the difference of t-score between characters [Sun et al. 1998]. The latter is used for determining whether to group $xy|z$ or $x|yz$ in a three-character sequence xyz. The t-score of character y relevant to character x and character z, denoted by $ts_{x,z}(y)$, is defined as in the Equation (4.2):

$$ts_{x,z}(y) = \frac{p(z|y) - p(y|x)}{\sqrt{\text{var}(p(z|y)) + \text{var}(p(y|x))}} \qquad (4.5)$$

where $p(z|y)$ denotes the conditional probability of z given y, and $\text{var}(p(z|y))$ denotes its variance [similarly for $p(y|x)$ and $\text{var}(p(y|x))$]. This measures the binding tendency of y in the context of x

and z: y tends to be bound with x if $ts_{x,z}(y)<0$ and with z if $ts_{x,z}(y)>0$. Further measures are used to determine the segmentation of longer sequences. The mutual information and t-score values are then combined to determine the best segmentation.

Ge et al. [1999] proposed a probabilistic model based on the Expectation Maximization (EM) algorithm. This model makes the following three assumptions:

1. There are a finite number of words of length 1 to k, (e.g., $k=4$).
2. Each word has an unknown probability of occurrence.
3. Words are independent of each other.

Here, the words are the candidate multi-grams from the training corpus. Word probabilities are randomly assigned initially, and they are used for segmenting the texts. The word probabilities are then re-estimated based on the segmentation results, and the texts are re-segmented using the re-estimated probabilities. The algorithm iterates until convergence.

2. Statistical dictionary-based approaches

Studies combining statistical and dictionary-based approaches attempt to benefit from both words. A good example of this approach is presented in Sproat et al. [1996], which used weighted finite state transducers for Chinese word segmentation. The model works as follows:

1. A dictionary is represented as a weighted finite state transducer. Each word is represented as a sequence of arcs that represent mappings between a character and its pronunciation. It is terminated by a weighted arc that represents the transduction in an empty string.
2. Weights on word strings represent their estimated cost. These are the negative log probabilities of the word-strings and are derived from frequencies of the strings in a 20M character corpus.
3. Represent input I as an unweighted acceptor over the set of Chinese characters.
4. Choose the path with the lowest cost as the best segmentation for the input.

The cost for a word w, $c(w)$, is computed as in Equation (4.3), where $f(w)$ denotes the frequency of the word in the corpus, and N denotes the size of the corpus.

$$c(w) = -\log\frac{f(w)}{N} \qquad (4.6)$$

This approach has also been implemented for derived words and person names in their system. It needs to have some mechanism to estimate the probabilities of different types of unknown words.

For example, for derived words, Church and Gale [1991] used the Good-Turing estimate, where the aggregate probability of unseen instances is estimated as n_1/N, where N is the size of the corpus, and n_1 is the number of types (of the construction) observed once. Let X denote a particular suffix, and unseen(X) denote the set of unseen derived words with suffix X, then the Good-Turing estimate gives an estimate of $p(\text{unseen}(X)|X)$, i.e., the probability of observing a previously unseen instance of a derived word with suffix X given that we know derived words with suffix X exist. However, other types of unknown words, e.g., "聊聊," are not catered for, and modeling the probabilities for other types of unknown words remains an unsolved problem for this framework. They mentioned that the only way to handle reduplicated words would be to expand out the reduplicated forms beforehand and incorporate those forms into the lexical transducer.

Peng and Schuurmans [2001] is another example of this approach. They proposed a variant of the EM algorithm for Chinese segmentation. This approach keeps a core lexicon which contains real words and a candidate lexicon that contains all other multi-grams not in the core lexicon. The EM algorithm is used to maximize the likelihood of the training corpus given the two lexicons and suggest new words as candidates for the core lexicon. Once new words are added to the core lexicon, the EM algorithm is reinitialized by giving half of the total probability mass to the core lexicon, allowing the words in the core lexicon to guide the segmentation. Once the EM has stabilized, then the mutual information was used to eliminate longer agglomerations in favor of shorter primitives, as maximum likelihood training tends to penalize segmentation with more chunks. These measures are taken to lead the EM algorithmm out of a poor local maximum. Ge at al [1999] proposed to segment unknown words while doing word segmentation. It reports that mutual information pruning yielded significant improvement, but they agree with Sproat et al. [1996] in saying that the quality of the base lexicon is perhaps more important than the model itself.

(c)   Comprehension-based approach

In the abovementioned work, each sentence is processed without employing any information about the previous sentences, so every sentence is considered separately from the text containing it. Some studies investigate the advantages arising from taking into account the syntactic structure of sentences. A comprehension-based approach was presented by Chen and Bai [1997], which used a segmented training corpus to learn a set of rules to discriminate monosyllabic words from monosyllabic morphemes that may be parts of unknown words. They consider monosyllabic words as instances of lexical units and component characters of unknown words that cannot be monosyllabic words as instances of nonlexical. Then they examine the instances lexical units and nonlexical units as well as their contexts in the corpus and derive a set of context-dependent rules. These rules are ranked according to their accuracy in identifying proper characters. The rules whose accuracy surpasses a predetermined threshold are sequentially applied to distinguish proper and improper characters. They report a best precision rate of 74.61% with 68.18% recall.

Chen and Ma [2002] extended the work. After identifying lexical units and nonlexical units, they used a set of context free morphological rules to model the structure of unknown words. Two example rules are given below:

Example 4.3.3: (a) UW → ms(?)ps(), (b) UW → UWps(),

where UW is short for "unknown word" which is the start symbol. The ms(?), ps(), and ms() are three terminal symbols, which stand for a monosyllable detected as a nonlexical unit, a monosyllable not detected as a nonlexical, and a multisyllabic known word, respectively. These rules are appended with the linguistic (e.g., restricting the syntactic category of a symbol) or the statistical (e.g., requiring a minimum frequency of a symbol) constraints to avoid excessive superfluous extractions. These rules are ranked by the association strength of their right-hand side symbols. Finally, they use a bottom-up merging algorithm that consults the morphological rules to extract unknown words. A precision of 76% and a recall of 57% are reported.

Further, Wu and Jiang [1988] presented a word segmentation method by using syntactic analysis. The authors proposed to segment words based on the syntactic parser. According to the study, the MM algorithm is excessively dependent upon the dictionary, and lacks global information, similarly, the statistical approach shows lack of the information of the sentence structure, which the syntactic parser can provide. Therefore, Wu and Jiang applied the technology of sentence understanding to word segmentation. However, adding syntactic parser into word segmentation cannot improve the precision dramatically in some experiments [Huang and Zhao 2007].

(d)   Machine learning-based approaches

With the availability of word-segmented training corpus, a number of supervised machine learning algorithms have been applied also to Chinese word segmentation. Given the large body of literature within this framework, this subsection introduces some of the most recent and successful studies using these approaches.

1.   Transformation-based algorithm

The transformation-based learning (TBL) algorithm [Bill 1995] is probably the first machine learning algorithm that has been applied to Chinese word segmentation [Palmer and Burger 1997; Hockenmaier and Brew 1998; Florian and Ngai 2001; Xue 2001]. This algorithm requires a pre-segmented reference corpus and an initial segmenter. The initial segmenter can be naive or sophisticated, e.g., it may simply treat every character as a word, or it could apply the MM algorithm. The initial segmenter is used to produce an initial segmentation of the unsegmented version of the reference corpus. In the first iteration, the learning algorithm compares the initial segmentation with the reference corpus and identifies a rule that, if applied, achieves the greatest gain based on some evaluation functions, e.g., the number of segmentation error reductions. The initial segmentation is updated by applying the rule, and the learning algorithm iterates until the maximum gain is below a predefined threshold and no significant improvement can be achieved by any additional rule. The algorithm outputs a set of ranked rules, which can be used to process new texts.

2.   Hidden Markov model

Another representative machine learning-based approach is presented in Ponte et al. [1996], which tries to apply the Hidden Markov Model (HMM) for Chinese word segmentation. This approach needs the information of part-of-speech (POS) tagging, which deals with word segmentation and POS tagging at the same time.

The approach is described in detail as follows. Let S be the given sentence (sequence of characters) and $S(W)$ be the sequence of characters that composes the word sequence W. POS tagging is defined as the determination of the POS tag sequence, $T=t_1, ..., t_n$, if a segmentation into a word sequence $W=w_1, ..., w_n$ is given. The goal is to find the POS sequence T and word sequence W that maximize the following probability:

$$
\begin{aligned}
W, T &= \arg \max_{W,T,W(S)=S} P(T, W \mid S) \\
&= \arg \max_{W,T,W(S)=S} P(W, T) \\
&= \arg \max_{W,T,W(S)=S} P(W \mid T) P(T)
\end{aligned}
\tag{4.7}
$$

We make the following approximations that the tag probability, $P(T)$, is determined by the preceding tag only and the conditional word probability, $P(W|T)$, is determined by the tag of the word. HMM assumes that each word is generating a hidden state which is the same as the POS tag of the word. A tag t_{i-1} transits to another tag t_i with the probability $P(t_i|t_{i-1})$ and outputs a word with the probability $P(w_i|t_i)$. Then the approximation for both probabilities can be rewritten as follows:

$$
P(W|T) \stackrel{\Delta}{=} \prod_{i=1}^{n} P(w_i \mid t_i)
\tag{4.8}
$$

$$
P(T) = \prod_{i=1}^{n} P(t_i \mid t_{i-1})
\tag{4.9}
$$

The probabilities are estimated from the frequencies of instances in a tagged corpus using maximum likelihood estimation. $F(X)$ is the frequency of instances in the tagged corpus, $<w_i, t_i>$ shows the co-occurrences of a word and a tag, and $<t_i, t_{i-1}>$ shows the co-occurrences of two tags.

$$P(w_i|t_i) = \frac{F(<w_i, t_i>)}{F(t_i)} \qquad (4.10)$$

$$P(t_i|t_{i-1}) = \frac{F(t_i, t_{i-1})}{F(t_{i-1})} \qquad (4.11)$$

The possible segmentation of a sentence can be represented by a lattice. The nodes in the lattice show possible words together with the POS tags. With the estimated parameters, the most probable tag and word sequence are determined using the Viterbi algorithm [Forney 1973]. In practice, negated log likelihood of $P(w_i|t_i)$ and $P(t_i|t_{i-1})$ is calculated as the cost. Maximizing the probability is equivalent to minimizing the cost.

This approach is only able to segment known words that can be found in the dictionary. If some words are not found in the dictionary, they will be segmented depending on the parts of words that can be found in the dictionary. However, unknown words detection needs to be done in a separate process.

3. Other algorithms

Gao et al. [2005] used source-channel models for Chinese word segmentation. They defined five word classes for their system, namely, lexicon words, morphologically derived words, factoids, named entities, and new words. In their system, each character sequence was segmented into a word class sequence, using the following basic form of source-channel models:

$$w^* = \underset{w \in \text{GEN}(s)}{\text{argmax}} \; P(w|s) = \underset{w \in \text{GEN}(s)}{\text{argmax}} \; P(w)P(s|w) \qquad (4.12)$$

where s denotes a character sequence, w denotes a word class sequence, GEN(s) denotes the set of all candidate word class sequences into which s could have been segmented, and w^* denotes the most likely word class sequence among all the candidates. This basic form of the source-channel models is generalized as linear mixture models that allow the system to incorporate a very large number of linguistic and statistical features. In such linear models, the likelihood of a word class sequence is written as in Equation (4.13), and Equation (4.12) is rewritten as in Equation (4.14):

$$\text{Score}(w, s, \lambda) = \sum_{d=0}^{D} \lambda_d f_d(w, s) \qquad (4.13)$$

$$w^* = \underset{w \in \text{GEN}(s)}{\text{argmax}} \; \text{Score}(w, s, \lambda) \qquad (4.14)$$

where $f_d(w, s)$ is the base feature defined as the logarithm probability of the word class trigram model, and $f_d(w, s)$, for $d=1...D$, is a feature function for word class d, which has weight λ_d. λ_d is estimated using the framework of gradient descent.

By now, we have discussed several approaches. There are some pros and cons with these approaches. The dictionary-based approach is easy to implement, which can ensure high precision for known word detection, but the recall is not quite satisfactory due to the difficulty of detecting new patterns of words. The statistics-based approach requires a large annotated corpus for training and the results turn out to be better. The comprehension approaches theoretically can achieve precision at 99%, but performed poorly in the Bakeoff. Therefore, in order to get optimum results, people are combining these approaches with some other methods, such as machine learning, which is currently the most popular approach.

4.4   WORD SEGMENTATION AMBIGUITY

The ambiguity is one of the main challenges in Chinese word segmentation, which has been studied by researchers for many years. By now, people have focused on the following different methods, which are dictionary-based method, statistics-based method, and some other methods as well. In this section, we will first give the formal definition of Chinese word segmentation ambiguity and then introduce each method in detail.

4.4.1   Ambiguity Definition

Some of the Chinese word segmentation ambiguity is generated by the overlapping of the characters string OAS, which is a Chinese character string O that satisfies the following two conditions [Li et al. 2003]:

   a.   There exist two segmentations Seg_1 and Seg_2 such that $\forall w_1 \in Seg_1$, $w_2 \in Seg_2$, where Chinese word w_1 and w_2 are different from either literal strings or positions.

   b. $\exists w_1 \in Seg_1$, $w_2 \in Seg_2$, where w_1 and w_2 overlap.

The first condition ensures that there are ambiguous word boundaries (if more than one word segmentor is applied) in an OAS. In Example 4.1(a), the string "各国有" is an OAS but "各国有企业" is not, because the word "企业" remains the same in both of "各|国有|企业" and "各国|有|企业". The second condition indicates that the ambiguous word boundaries result from crossing brackets, and words "各国" and "国有" form a crossing bracket.

Example 4.4.1: (a) 在各国有企业中，技术要求强的岗位数量在不断增加。 (b) 在人民生活水平问题上，各国有共同点。

The longest OAS is an OAS that is not a substring of any other OAS in a given sentence. In Example 4.4.1(b), "生活水平" (living standard), both "生活" and "生活水平" are OASs, but only "生活水平" is the longest OAS because "生活" is a substring of "生活水平".

4.4.2   Disambiguation Algorithms

(a)   Dictionary-based method

The intuition of solving the ambiguity problem is applying a dictionary-based approach. The maximum matching (MM) algorithm is regarded as the simplest dictionary-based word segmentation approach. It starts from one end of a sentence and tries to match the first longest word wherever possible. Looking at the outputs produced by FMM and BMM, we can determine the places where overlapping ambiguities occur. For example, FMM will segment the string "即将来临时" (when the time comes) into "即将/来临/时/" (immediately/come/when), but BMM will segment it into "即/将来/临时/" (that/future/temporary).

Let O_f and O_b be the outputs of FMM and BMM, respectively. In Huang [1997], for overlapping cases, if $O_f = O_b$, then the probability that both the MMs will be the correct answer is 99%. If $O_f \neq O_b$, then the probability that either O_f or O_b will be the correct answer is also 99%. However, for covering ambiguity cases, even if $O_f = O_b$, both O_f and O_b could be either correct or wrong. If there are any unknown words, they would normally be segmented as single characters by both FMM and BMM.

Therefore, the overlapping ambiguity resolution can be formulized as a binary classification problem as follows:

Given a longest OAS O and its context feature set $C = \{w_{-m} \ldots w_{-1}, w_1 \ldots w_n\}$, let $G(\text{Seg}, C)$ be a score function of Seg for $\text{seg} \in \{O_f, O_b\}$, the overlapping ambiguity resolution task is to make the binary decision:

$$\text{seg} \begin{cases} O_f & G(O_f, C) > G(O_b, C) \\ O_b & G(O_f, C) < G(O_b, C) \end{cases} \tag{4.15}$$

$$G = p(\text{Seg}) \prod_{i=m\cdots-1,1\cdots n} p(wi | \text{Seg}) \tag{4.16}$$

Note that $O_f = O_b$ means that both FMM and BMM arrive at the same result. The classification process can then be stated as:

(a)   If $O_f = O_b$, then choose either segmentation result since they are same.

(b)   Otherwise, choose the one with the higher score G according to Equation (4.15).

For example, in the example of "搜索引擎," if $O_f=O_b$="搜索|引擎," then "搜索|引擎" is selected as the answer. In another example of "各国有" in Example 4.4.1(b), O_f="各国|有," O_b="各|国有". Assume that C={在, 企业}, i.e., using a context window of size 3; then the segmentation "各国|有" is selected if G("各国|有," {在, 企业})>G("各|国有," {在, 企业}), otherwise "各|国有" is selected.

Dictionary-based method is a greedy algorithm, but it has been empirically proved to achieve over 90% accuracy if the dictionary is large. However, it is impossible to detect unknown words because only those words existing in the dictionary can be segmented correctly.

(b)   Statistics-based method

Vector space model (VSM) [Salton and Buckley 1988] is a typical statistics-based method to solve the word segmentation disambiguity (WSD) problem [Luo et al. 2002]. In VSM, the vector space is used to formulate contexts of polysemous words [Yarowsky 1992; Gale et al. 1993; Ide and Veronis 1998], and the contexts of ambiguous words are necessary for the resolution of covering ambiguities.

In VSM, all words co-occurring with an ambiguous word w could be extracted from sentences to form the vector of w, serving as its context. Xiao et al. [2001] found that it was appropriate to resolve covering ambiguity if the context window is restricted to ±3 words centered on w. For example, three words preceding w and three words following w in Figure 4.2. The position of a neighboring word of w is indicated in a negative number if it is on the left side of w and positive on the right side. Xiao et al. [2001] suggested that disambiguation would be more effective if the six words are further divided into four regions, namely, R_1 for w_{-3} and w_{-2}, R_2 for w_{-1}, R_3 for w_{+1}, and R_4 for w_{+2} and w_{+3}.

To fit the task, the variables are restated in Table 4.1. Given an ambiguous word w, let the segmentation form i of w be: $i=1$ (when w=the combined form), $i=2$ (when w=separated form).

To compute the weight of the word t_j in region R_k for the segmentation form i of w, the general form ($i=1, 2; j=1...n; k=1...4$) are defined as follows:

$$TF_{ijk}=tf_{ijk}$$
$$IDF_{jk}=idf_{jk}=log(d/df_{jk}) \tag{4.17}$$

在 社会 发展 中将 起到 关键 作用

$$\underbrace{w_{-3} \quad w_{-2}}_{R1} \quad \underbrace{w_{-1}}_{R2} \quad w \quad \underbrace{w_{+1}}_{R3} \quad \underbrace{w_{+2} \quad w_{+3}}_{R4}$$

FIGURE 4.2: The window of context of w.

TABLE 4.1: Definition of variables	
D	The number of segmentation forms of w. It is always 2.
D_i	The collection of sentences containing w in the segmentation form i (the training set of w).
n	The number of distinct words in the union of D_1 and D_2.
tf_{ijk}	The frequency of word t_j in region R_k in collection D_i.
tf_{qjk}	The frequency of word t_j in region R_k in the input sentence Q containing w.
df_{jk}	The number of collections (D_1 and D_2) that contain t_j in region R_k. Its value ranges from 0 to 2.
idf_{jk}	$\log(d/df_{jk})$

The similarity coefficient (SC) between w in the input sentence Q and the segmentation form i of w is defined as:

$$\text{SC}(Q, i) = \sum_{j=1}^{n} \sum_{k=1}^{4} tf_{qij} \times d_{ijk} \qquad (4.18)$$

The ambiguous word w in Q will take the segmentation form that maximizes Equation (4.18) over i.

The VSM is high-dimensional due to the large number of words in Chinese lexicon, so it encounters a serious data sparseness problem. To solve this, a Chinese thesaurus 《同义词词林》 [Mei et al. 1983] is used. A reasonable strategy here would be to replace low frequency words in vector space with their semantic codes. A consequence of doing so is that the generalization capability of the model may also be improved to some extent.

Besides, there are some models in rule-based methods [Huang et al. 1997], which use few rules to predict the semantic categories of OAS based on syntactic and semantic categories. These rule-based methods have some regularities for the data that can be captured in a more direct and effective way. A separate set of rules are developed for words that are two-, three-, and four-character long.

4.5 BENCHMARKS

4.5.1 Standards

In this subsection, we briefly review three influential Chinese word segmentation standards that have been adopted in three independent large-scale corpus construction projects.

1.   Peking University standard

Yu et al. [2002] described the segmentation standard adopted for the Contemporary Chinese Corpus developed at Peking University. This standard is characterized by a large set of specific rules. Each rule explains how a particular kind of character string should be segmented. The grammatical knowledge-base of contemporary Chinese [Yu et al. 2001b], a lexicon with over 73,000 unique entries, is used as a reference lexicon for segmentation. In general, all entries in the lexicon are treated as one segmentation unit.

2.   Academia Sinica standard

Huang et al. [1997] described the segmentation standard adopted for the Sinica Corpus developed by Academia Sinica in Taiwan. This standard also assumes the use of a reference lexicon for segmentation. Unlike the Peking University standard, the Academia Sinica standard does not have a large set of specific rules, but a definition for segmentation unit, two segmentation principles, and four specific segmentation guidelines. A segmentation unit is defined as the smallest string of characters with an independent meaning and a fixed grammatical category.

3.   University of Pennsylvania standard

Xia [2000] described the segmentation standard adopted for the Penn Chinese Treebank developed at the University of Pennsylvania, USA. This standard is very much like the Peking University Standard in the sense that it also consists of a large set of specific rules. Each rule specifies how a particular kind of character string should be handled. However, different from the two standards discussed above, this standard does not assume the use of any reference lexicon for segmentation. Therefore, the annotator cannot assume any character string to be known, but needs to determine the wordhood status for each character string. To make this possible, the rules in the standard attempt to cover all possible scenarios, and the set become inevitably large.

4.5.2   Bakeoff Evaluation

The "Bakeoff evaluation" first held at the 2nd SIGHAN Workshop at ACL in 2003 [Sproat and Emerson 2003] has become the preeminent measure for Chinese word segmentation evaluation. The purpose is to compare the accuracy of various methods. As far as we know, there is no uniform standard of Chinese word segmentation. A text can be segmented differently depending on the linguists who decide on the rules and also the purpose of the segmentation. Therefore, this Bakeoff intends to standardize the training and testing Corpora, so that a fair evaluation could be made. There are two tracks in the Bakeoff: open and closed. In the open track, the participants are allowed to use any other resources such as dictionaries or more training data in their system besides the training materials provided. However, in the closed track, the condition is somewhat stricter, and no other material other than the training data provided is allowed to be used to train the system.

The results of SIGHAN Bakeoff are evaluated in five measurements: recall, precision, and *F*-measure for overall segmentation, and recall for unknown words and known words, as shown in the equations below.

$$\text{Recall} = \frac{\text{number of correctly segmented words}}{\text{total number of words in gold data}}$$

$$\text{Precision} = \frac{\text{number of correctly segmented words}}{\text{total number of words segmented}}$$

$$F - \text{measure} = \frac{2 \times \text{Recall} \times \text{Precision}}{\text{Recall} + \text{Precision}}$$

$$\text{Recall (OOV)} = \frac{\text{number of correctly segmented unknown words}}{\text{total number of unknown words in gold data}}$$

$$\text{Recall (IV)} = \frac{\text{number of correctly segmented known words}}{\text{total number of known words in gold data}}$$

The fourth bakeoff augmented the words segmentation task with a new named entity recognition task. The following tasks will be evaluated:

- Chinese word segmentation,
- Chinese named entity recognition, and
- Chinese POS tagging.

The Corpora are provided by seven different institutions. They are Academia Sinica, City University of Hong Kong, Microsoft Research Asia, Peking University, Shanxi University, State Language Commission of PRC, Beijing (National Chinese Corpus), and University of Colorado, USA (Chinese Tree Bank).

4.6   FREE TOOLS

During the last decade, there are many Chinese word segmentation systems developed by some institutes and universities. In this section, we just mainly want to describe two systems, namely, the Institute of Computing Technology, Chinese Lexical Analysis System (ICTCLAS) and the Microsoft Research Segmenter (MSRSeg) system.

4.6.1 Chinese Lexical Analysis System

ICTCLAS is developed by the Institute of Computing Technology [ICT 2008], and it is well known as the most popular Chinese word segmentation system. ICTCLAS is composed of five functional modules, namely, Chinese word segmentation, POS tagging, named entity recognition, unknown words detection, and the user-defined dictionary. The core of ICTCLAS has been updated for six times during the last 5 years, and the current version is ICTCLAS 2008, which can improve the speed of word segmentation to 996 kbps with the precision of 98.45%. Besides, the application programming interface (API) of ICTCLAS 2008 is less than 200 kb, and the total size of the whole dictionary is smaller than 3 MB after compression. In the Bakeoff of SIGHAN throughout the previous years, ICTCLAS won the first place for many times.

4.6.2 MSRSeg System

MSRSeg[1] is developed by the Natural Language Computing Group at Microsoft Research Asia. MSRSeg consists of two components: (1) a generic segmenter (based on the framework of linear mixture models, which is composed of four modules: the sentence segmenter, the word candidate generator, the decoder, and the wrapper) and (2) a set of output adaptors (for adapting the output of the former to different application-specific standards). The MSRSeg System was first released in 2004, and during the last couple of years, it was augmented with new functions from year to year. The current version is able to provide a unified approach to the five fundamental features of word-level Chinese language processing: lexicon word processing, morphological analysis, factoid detection, named entity recognition, and new word identification [Gao et al. 2005] (see also Chapter 3.3.1).

S-MSRSeg System, a simplified version of MSRSeg can be downloaded from [MSRA 2008], which only provides some of the functions, and does not provide the functionalities of new word identification, morphology analysis, and standards adaptation.

4.7 SUMMARY

This chapter gives an overview of Chinese word segmentation. Firstly, we compare the differences between Chinese and English and give a formal definition of Chinese word segmentation. We then enlist some real-world examples to highlight the two main challenges, i.e., ambiguity and unknown words. After that, we give a classification of word segmentation approaches and discuss the details of different specific algorithms. We also introduce three standards for Chinese word segmentation evaluation and the Bakeoff in SIGHAN. Finally, we present a few free tools for Chinese word segmentation.

· · · · ·

---

[1]The MSRSeg is not an open code tool, and it can be downloaded from the Microsoft Website.

CHAPTER 5

Unknown Word Identification

5.1 INTRODUCTION

Dictionary-based method is popular for word segmentation. A pre-compiled dictionary is the prerequisite for this method. However, a dictionary is inevitably a closed system. It is comprised of a finite set of vocabulary. However, in a natural language system, new words and phrases are coined almost daily. As such, words that come in after the creation of the dictionary will not be included in the vocabulary list. The existence of unknown word in a dictionary is commonly referred to as the Out Of Vocabulary (OOV) problem in dictionary-based NLP applications, e.g., information retrieval (IR) [Jin and Wong 2002], and word segmentation application is no exception.

Recent studies show that more than 60% of word segmentation errors result from unknown word. Statistics also show that more than 1,000 new Chinese words appear every year. These words are mostly domain-specific technical terms, e.g., 视窗 (windows) and time-sensitive political/social/cultural terms, e.g., 三个代表 (Three Represents Theory), 非典 (SARS), and 海归 (expatriate students). In practice, even if these terms are recognized, they are often not added to the dictionary.

Unknown word come in different forms including proper nouns (person names, organization names, place names, etc.), domain-specific terminological nouns and abbreviations, made-up terms (e.g., those found in blogs), etc. They appear frequently in real text and affect the performance of automatic Chinese word segmentation. Due to an unknown word, a sentence can be inappropriately segmented into incorrect word sequences. Therefore, effective unknown word detection and recognition are fundamental to word segmentation.

However, it is difficult to identify an unknown word because almost all Chinese characters can be either a morpheme or a word. Even worse, most morphemes are polysemous. These allow new words to be constructed easily by combining morphemes and words. In general, there are two ways to generate new words, namely, compounding and affixation [Tseng 2003].

1. *Compounding.* A compound is a word made up of other words. In general, Chinese compounds are made up of words that are linked together by morpho-syntactic relations such as modifier–head, verb–object, and so on. For example, 光幻觉 (optical illusion) consists of 光 (light) and 幻觉 (illusion), and the relation is modifier–head. 光过敏 (photosensitization) is made up of 光 (light) and 过敏 (allergy), and the relation is modifier–head.

2. *Affixation.* A word is formed by affixation when a stem is combined with a prefix or a suffix morpheme. For example, English suffixes such as *-ian* and *-ist* are used to create words referring to a person with a specialty, such as "musician" and "scientist." Such suffixes can give very specific evidence for the semantic class of the word. Chinese has suffixes with similar meanings to -ian or -ist such as the Chinese suffix -家 (*-jia*). However, the Chinese affix is a much weaker cue to the semantic category of the word than English -ist or -ian, because it is more ambiguous. The suffix -家 (*-jia*) contains three major concepts: (1) expert, e.g., 科学家 (scientist) and 音乐家 (musician); (2) family and home, e.g., 全家 (whole family) and 富贵家 (rich family); and (3) house, e.g., 搬家 (to move house). In English, the meaning of an unknown word with the suffix -ian or -ist is clear; however, in Chinese, an unknown word with the suffix -家 (*-jia*) could have multiple interpretations. Another example of ambiguous suffix, -性 (*-xing*), has three main concepts: (1) gender, e.g., 女性 (female); (2) property, such as 药性 (property of a medicine), 3) a characteristic, 嗜杀成 性 (a characteristic of being bloodthirsty). Even though Chinese also has morphological suffixes to generate new words, they do not determine meaning and syntactic category as clearly as they do in English.

In practice, unknown word can be of different types. The previously mentioned compounds and affixations are categorized as compounds and derived words, respectively, by Chen and Ma [1998], who observed the following five types of unknown word that most frequently occur in the Sinica Corpus:

1. Abbreviation (acronym): It is difficult to identify abbreviations since their morphological structures are very irregular. Their affixes more or less reflect the conventions of the selection of meaning components. However, the affixes of abbreviations are common words which are least informative for indicating the existence of unknown word.

2. Proper names: Proper names can be further classified into three common sub-categories, i.e., names of people, names of places, and names of organizations. Certain keywords are indicators for each different sub-category. For instance, there are about 100 common surnames which are prefix characters of Chinese personal names. The district names, such as "city," "country," etc., frequently occurs as suffixes of the names of places. Identification of company names is as difficult as that of abbreviations since there is no restriction on the choice of morpheme components.

3. Derived words: Derived words have affix morphemes which are strong indicators.

4. Compounds: A compounds is a very productive type of unknown word. Nominal and verbal compounds are easily coined by combining two words/characters. Since there are more

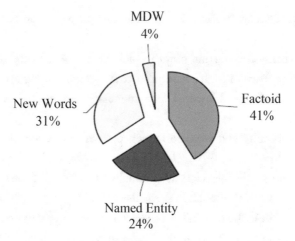

FIGURE 5.1: The percentage of each unknown word type.

than 5,000 commonly used Chinese characters, each with idiosyncratic syntactic behavior, it is hard to derive a set of morphological rules to generate the set of Chinese compounds. To identify Chinese compounds is, thus, also difficult.

5. Numeric type compounds: The characteristic of numeric compounds is that they contain numbers as their major components. For instance, dates, time, phone numbers, addresses, numbers, determiner–measure compounds, etc., belong to this type. Since digital numbers are the major components of unknown word of this type and their morphological structures are more regular, they can be identified using morphological rules.

Similarly categorization was also presented by Gao et al. [2005], which have defined four types of unknown word including morphologically derived words, factoids (e.g., date, time, percentage, money, number, measure, email, phone number, and URL), named entities (NE, e.g., person name, location names and organization name), and other new words, of which, new words refer those time-sensitive concepts or domain-specific terms. The percentages of each type are illustrated below (see Fig. 5.1).

5.2   UNKNOWN WORD DETECTION AND RECOGNITION

The approaches to unknown (new) word recognition range from rule-based approaches to statistics-based and learning-based approaches. Regardless of the approaches used, the goal is basically to decide whether a character string is a dictionary word or not and whether an OOV string can form a word or not. Information normally used for unknown word recognition include frequency and relative frequency, in-word probability (i.e., the probability of a character being inside a word), word-formation pattern, mutual information [Church and Hanks 1990], left/right entropy [Sornlertlamvanich et al. 2000], context dependency [Chien 1999], independent words probability [Nie et al. 1995], anti-word list, etc.

Frequency is normally the starting point to pick up new word candidates. A string of characters that has a high frequency or high co-occurrence frequency among other components is often treated as a new word candidate. However, low-frequency new words are hardly identifiable by statistical methods.

Both in-word probability and word-formation pattern reflect the morphological property of Chinese. For example, Chen et al. [2005], Wu and Jiang [2000], and Fu [2001] used in-word probability to combine adjacent single characters after initial segmentation if the product of their in-word probability is larger than a preset threshold. In particular, Wu and Jiang [2000] and Fu [2001] also used word-formation pattern to describe how likely a character appears in a certain position within a word.

Cohesiveness measures, such as mutual information, estimates the internal association strength among constituents of character n-grams which are likely new word candidates. Both left/right entropy and context dependency describe the dependency strength of current items (character sequence) on its context. The dependency strength of a current item on its context decreases as the probability of this item to be a Chinese word increases.

The process of recognition can be naturally divided into two steps: candidate detection and unknown word recognition. The task in the second step is to verify or eliminate the candidates that are detected in the first step.

Many people, such as Wu and Jiang [2000], tried to identify unknown words, which were composed by multiple characters words. Therefore, if a sequence of single characters (not subsumed by any words) is found after the completion of basic word segmentation and name identification, this sequence is very likely to be a new word. This basic intuition has been extensively discussed. However, not every character sequence is a word in Chinese. Thus, only those sequences of single characters where the characters are unlikely to be a sequence of existing words are good candidates for new words.

The independent word probability is a property of a single character or a string of characters. The independent word probability of a single character is the likelihood for this character to appear as an independent word in texts, which is defined as:

$$IWP(c) = \frac{N(Word(c))}{N(c)} \qquad (5.1)$$

where $N(Word(c))$ is the number of occurrences of a character as an independent word in the sentences of a given text corpus, and $N(c)$ is the total number of occurrences of this character in the same corpus.

On the other hand, Li et al. [2004] and Nie et al. [1995] proposed to use an anti-word list, i.e., a list of functional characters, to exclude bad candidates. For example, the unknown word candidates which contain functional characters (e.g., single-character prepositional, adverbial, and conjunctive words, etc.) should be eliminated. Cui et al. [2006] conducted extensive study on garbage string detection for candidate filtering. They design different filtering mechanisms to separate the true new words from the garbage strings, using various new word patterns. The garbage strings, garbage lexicons, garbage heads, and garbage tails are learned automatically from the corpus.

It should be pointed out that Li et al. [2004] also investigated the analogy between new words and dictionary words. The hypothesis of the analogy between new words and dictionary words is: if two characters appear more times in the same word patterns, the analogy between them is more reliable. For example, 下 (below) has the most identical word patterns with 上 (above), and there is a strong preference for them to produce analogous words. The equation below shows the valuating principle, where a, c, x each represents a Chinese character. $C(.)$ is the number of occurrences in a corpus, given that the variable is a word.

$$ANA\,(a,x) = \frac{\sum_c [W(ac)\,W(xc) + W(ca)\,W(cx)]}{\sum_c [W(ac) + W(ca) + W(xc) + W(cx)]} \tag{5.2}$$

$$W(a,c) = \begin{cases} 1 \text{ or } C(ac), & \text{if } ac \text{ is in dictionary} \\ 0 & \text{otherwise} \end{cases} \tag{5.3}$$

While traditionally unknown word recognition has been considered a standalone process using a non-iterative segmentation detection paradigm, Peng et al. [2004] considered new word detection an integral part of segmentation, aiming to improve both segmentation and new word recognition interactively. The detected new words are added to the dictionary in order to improve segmentation accuracy. The augmented dictionary, which includes potential unknown words (in addition to known words), is then used in the next iteration of resegmentation. The improved segmentation result can thus further improve the next iteration of unknown word recognition.

Since there are many types of unknown words, it is not possible to find a uniform schema and categorization algorithm to handle all of them. Different clues can be used to identify different types of unknown word. For example, identification of people names is very much dependent on the surnames, which is a limited set of characters. Therefore, some researches especially focus on a particular types of named entities, mainly person names, place names, and organization names.

5.3 CHINESE PERSON NAME IDENTIFICATION

A person name in Chinese is composed of a family name followed by a given name and both family and given names can be one or two characters long. According to statistics based on the People Daily Corpus, Chinese person names constitute more than one quarter of all OOV words.

In addition to the challenging issues with its English counterpart, Chinese person name identification also exhibits the following difficulties. First, name formation is arbitrary, i.e., there are not many rules or patterns to follow. Second, a name does not have "boundary tokens" such as the capitalized initial letters as in English. Third, different news agencies and people in different areas may translate the same foreign name to different Chinese names [Gao et al. 2004; Gao and Wong 2006].

Chinese person name identification is basically driven by family name. Although there are as many as 5,662 family names in all of ancient and modern Chinese literature, no more than 300 family names are commonly used nowadays. There are some existing family name dictionaries and statistics of the family name characters on the Internet, "千家姓" (http://pjoke.com/showxing.php), and published books such as "百家姓总汇," "姓氏词典," "中国古今姓氏词典," "中华姓氏大辞典," and "姓氏人名用字分析统計," etc.

As compared with family name identification, which has already achieved relatively high recall and precision by simply using a pre-compiled family name dictionary, identification of given names is more difficult due to two reasons. First, the choice of the characters used in a given name is more random and disperse. Second, the characters in a given name can be ordinary words by themselves, or the combination with adjacent characters can form ordinary words. Some interesting examples are illustrated in Table 1.

Therefore, the name identification problem becomes the detection of the name's right boundaries. For a quick solution, one can make use of the fact that most given names are either 1 or 2 in length

TABLE 5.1: Examples of Chinese names with different characters

TYPES OF ORDINARY WORDS IN NAMES	EXAMPLES
Two-character name	高峰, 文静
Three-character name	黄灿灿
The first two characters	刘海亮, 黄金荣
The last two characters	朱俊杰, 叶海燕

as the clue for identifying the right boundary positions. However, for higher accuracy, one cannot simply rely on the name structure. One must take into account the characters which are widely used for name formation and the words/characters on the left and right side of the name under investigation.

Name is practically a special kind of noun in Chinese, hence like the other kinds of nouns, its identification can be improved by contextual information. Many studies constructed manually left context word list, including the words that indicate the appearance of the person names on their right-hand side. Examples include title words, such as "总理" (prime minister), "厂长" (factory manager), etc., and some verbs that are normally followed by person names such as "授予" (present), "接见" (meet), "称赞" (praise), etc. Some also use the patterns that contain both left and right context words flanking the names such as "以…为," "任命…为," "记者…报道," etc.

Often, a list of family names, a list of characters used in single character names, a list of characters used as the first character in two-character names, a list of characters used as the second character in two-character names, a list of titles, and a list of name prefix, such as "老" and "小," are collected manually or automatically from an annotated corpus. The statistics of different uses of the characters are also maintained if possible. These lists together with their statistics can then be used as rules in rule-based approaches [Luo and Song 2004] or as features in probability-based approaches [Wang and Yao 2003; Zhang and Liu 2004; Zhang et al. 2006]. Note also that these systems clearly show that dictionaries play an important role in person name identification.

As we have mentioned previously, a radical is the primary component of a Chinese character. Radicals can be roughly classified into semantic radicals and phonetic radicals. A semantic radical conveys the range or some aspect of the meaning of the whole character and thus has the potential to provide cues for the meaning of the whole character. A phonetic radical is often related to the pronunciation of the whole character. There are some interesting studies that try to explore the correlation between semantic radicals and Chinese characters used in given names so that the person name recognition algorithms could use these semantic radicals as computation resources.

Naming is very important in Chinese traditional culture. Some culture factors in naming can be well embodied in semantic radicals of given name characters. For example, people are apt to choose characters with radicals "玉" (jade and virtue) and "马" (horse) in given names. The gender difference in naming is also reflected in semantic radicals. Character with radicals "女" (female) and "草" (grass) are widely used in female names.

As mentioned before, one of the difficulties in Chinese name identification is how to recognize translated foreign names. Foreign names are usually transliterated from the pronunciations in the original languages [Gao et al. 2004; Gao and Wong 2006]. They can be any lengths, which poses a great challenge in identifying these names. Fortunately, there are some Chinese characters that appear particularly often in person name transliterations such as 尔 (*eri*), 姆 (*mu*), and 斯 (*si*). These characters typically do not carry obvious meanings and are normally not considered as common Chinese words. Other characters may be commonly used in other contexts in addition to that in transliterated foreign names. For example, the character 克 (*ke*) frequently appears as a part of a transliterated person name, but on the other hand, it also often forms many common Chinese words with other characters such as the word 克服 (overcome). In this case, contextual information must be used to resolve ambiguities.

5.4   CHINESE ORGANIZATION NAME IDENTIFICATION

Chinese organization name identification is considered to be a harder task as compared with the identification of person names, location names, and other types of unknown word because there are not many clues to indicate an organization name.

(a)   Difficulty

1. Compared with person names, the rules of organization name composition are complex. The only clear clues are the organization types.
2. Unlike person names, organization names have no predictable length. The length of an organization name varies from 2 to dozens of characters.
3. Organization names embody many other types of names. The majority of the embedded names are location names, in which most are unknown location names. The accuracy of organization name identification is thus largely conditioned on the accuracy of location name identification.
4. Words included in organization names are diverse. According to some statistics, 19,986 unique words in 10,817 organization names are of 27 different POS tags. Among them, nouns rank at the top, followed by location names. This problem is much more serious than other types of names.
5. Many organization names have abbreviations, which usually omit the part denoting organization type such as "微软 (Microsoft)" and "宏基电脑 (Acer Computer)." Some of them even have more than one abbreviation. Therefore, the task becomes not only identifying organization names in different forms but also finding their abbreviations. This makes organization name identification more challenging.

(b)   Internal structure of Chinese organization name

There is no rigid internal structure for an organization name. Roughly speaking, a Chinese organization name is composed of two major components. The first part is the proper name and the second part is the organization type. Organization types, such as 公司 (company), 基金会 (foundation), and 大学 (University), etc., clearly indicate what kinds of organizations they are. Therefore, the second part contains the major clue words that guide the identification of organization names, especially the identification of the right boundaries of organization names. That is why the organization types are sometimes called the organization name characteristic words and meanwhile the first part is called prefix words. Fortunately, although words used in the first part can be unlimited, the number of different organization types is limited. Determining the left boundaries then becomes most crucial to organization name identification. Most existing approaches either focus on determining the left boundary, or the possible composition of an organization name based on linguistic analysis and/or statistic properties, or attempt to filter out impossible ones from the potential organization name candidates by using organization name exclusive words/POS-tag constraints.

(c)   Features used for organization name composition

Given a corpus of sufficient size, one can obtain the probability of every word or character appearing or not appearing in an organization name. The words/characters appearing in organization names can more often be used to construct the organization word/character list. Many word lists, such as famous organization names and their abbreviations, are also considered as features.

(d)   Features used for potential left boundary identification

Many left boundary words are either (1) location name, e.g., 北京饭店 (Beijing Hotel) which indicates that the hotel is in Beijing City; (2) organization name, e.g., 北京大学数学学院 (School of Mathematical Science, Peking University), in which 北京大学 (Peking University) is the higher authority of 数学学院 (School of Mathematical Science); or (3) special word, e.g., "NEC."

(e)   Constraints used for organization name composition

Some "stop words," such as 失败 (failure) and 其它 (others), will never be selected as part of the name according to Chinese naming habits. Based on these observations, many recognition approaches have been designed. These approaches can be categorized into rule-based approaches [Chen and Chen 2000; Zhang et al. 2008] and probability-based approaches [Sun et al. 2003; Wu et al. 2003; Yu et al. 2003a].

It is worth mentioning that the role-based tagging approach was introduced by Yu et al. [2003a]. They defined a total of 11 roles for the tokens after segmentation and POS tagging, including organization name context words, organization name characteristic words, organization name exclusive words, and several kinds of prefix words. As a result, the identification of organization names is reduced to the role-tagging problem.

With the rapid growing Internet technology, Web pages have become an increasingly important data source for information extraction. Usually, name identification approaches focusing on plain text gives poor results on Web pages. Zhang et al. [2008] explored the differences between plain texts and Web pages. Based on the characteristic of hypertext markup language (HTML) structure, (1) important entities are often separated by Web page creators; (2) a Web page has a hierarchical structure and is useful for determining the association between recognized entities, otherwise it will be very difficult to associate them with plain text; and (3) in Web pages, important organization names often appear repeatedly in different locations such as title, Meta data, link anchor texts, etc. The algorithms they used are rule-based.

Organization name abbreviations are normally created from organization full names according to some construction conventions. Here are some examples:

1. Select the first character of the each word in an organization full name, e.g., 华东师范大学 (East China Normal University)→华师大.
2. If there is a proper name in an organization full name, select the proper name, e.g., 美国耐克公司 (America Nike Co.)→耐克 (Nike).
3. If an organization full name begins with a location name, select the location name plus the first character of the other words in the full name, e.g., 上海交通大学 (Shanghi Jiaotong University)→上海交大.
4. Select the words from the organization full name other than from the location name and the organization name characteristic word, e.g., 中国南方航空公司 (China Southern Airlines Company)→南方航空.
5. Select the first character of the words in an organization full name other than the location name and the organization name characteristic word, e.g., 中国南方航空公司 (China Southern Airlines Company)→南航.
6. Select the first character of all the words excluding the organization name characteristic word plus the organization name characteristic word, e.g., 交通银行总部 (Headquarter of Jiatong Bank)→交行总部.

These conventions can be used to identify organization name abbreviations based on the already identified organization full names.

5.5   CHINESE PLACE NAME RECOGNITION

The automatic recognition of Chinese place names is another case of the recognition of proper nouns in Chinese. The simplest way to do so is to build a place name dictionary and perform the dictionary lookup. The Chinese Place Name Set published by Place Names Committee of China is an example of such a dictionary. Other resources include中華人民共和國地名詞典, 中国古今地名大词典, and 中文地名索引, etc. Although Chinese Place Name Set includes nearly 100,000 place names, Zheng et al. [2001] showed that about 30% of the place names in a real text cannot be found. New place names emerge along with the development of economy and society.

Moreover, people sometimes select place names as the given names, such as "赵重庆" (Zhao Chongqing), to remember their birth places. In this example, Zhao is a typical family name and the given name Congcing is the name of a Chinese city. This is similar to the given name Sydney in English. To overcome this problem, the combination of corpus statistics and context rules plays an important role in Chinese place name recognition.

Corpus-based approaches normally estimate the likelihood of a character being a part of a Chinese place name (whether it is used as the beginning, middle, and end character) from the annotated corpus. This kind of likelihood can capture the capability of a character forming Chinese place names and thus provide a good means to locate the place name candidates. The candidates can then be confirmed or eliminated by applying context rules obtained by human observations from a large number of place name examples or by machine learning. The following are two examples of the confirmation and elimination rules:

1. If two place name candidates are coordinated and one is confirmed as a true place name, then the other should be confirmed as a true place name also.
2. A place name candidate should be eliminated if its preceding word is a tile of a person.

Compared with the publications on the recognition of other types of names, work on place names recognition is quite limited.

5.6   SUMMARY

This chapter presents the unknown word also called OOV problem in Chinese word segmentation. The problem is caused by the introduction of new words, which are not registered in the dictionary, i.e., a list of known words. If such a dictionary is used for word segmentation, performance will inevitably be affected.

Proper nouns representing person, place, and organization names are common sources of unknown word. Methods for name recognition are introduced. These methods make use of clues such as common naming structure, characters regularly used for names, contextual information, etc. These clues are obtained by either manual or automatic extraction from corpus.

· · · · ·

CHAPTER 6

Word Meaning

6.1 BASIC MEANING, CONCEPT, AND RELATION

In the previous chapters, our attention was mainly on the structure of words. No less important, however, especially in the case of Chinese, is word meaning and its linguistic and extralinguistic context. Without making use of the meaning in its broader sense, it is impossible to solve many problems in NLP such as WSD, correct syntactic parsing, sentence comprehension, information extraction, and machine translation. Therefore, this chapter is devoted to the exposition of word meaning including basic meaning concepts and their relations, the contextual notions of frame, collocation and verb valency, and the semantic resources used in the NLP of Chinese, such as dictionaries/lexicons and knowledge bases, including CILIN, HowNet, and Chinese Concept Dictionary (CCD). The following are some basic semantic concepts and the relations between words, which are universal to English and Chinese:

> *Sense/semantics/meaning*: they are all used to refer to meaning.
> *Sememe* 义元: the smallest unit of meaning and is not further divisible (e.g., the sememe <move> is shared by the various action morphemes *walk, run, roll, jump*, etc.).
> *Homonyms* 同音: words with different meanings, but they are pronounced in the same way (e.g., *bank* represents at least two homonyms, i.e., as a financial institution and as in riverbank).
> *Polysemes* 多义: words or phrases with multiple, related meanings (e.g., *bed* can be used in river bed as well as in bed as a household furniture).
> *Synonyms* 同义: different words having similar or identical meanings (e.g., *student* and *pupil*; *buy* and *purchase*, etc.).
> *Synset*: a set of one or more synonyms.
> *Antonyms* 反义: different words having contradictory or contrary meanings. For example, *perfect* and *imperfect* are contradictory, because if it is not perfect then it is imperfect; but *big* and *small* are contrary to each other, because something can be neither big nor small.
> *Hypernymy* 上位: the semantic relation of being superordinate or belonging to a higher rank or class (e.g., "living things" is a hypernym of "human").

> *Hyponomy* 下位: the opposite of *hypernymy*; the semantic relation of being subordinate or belonging to a lower rank or class. For example, "adult" is a hyponom of "human."

> *Holonymy* 整体: a word that defines the relationship between a term denoting the whole and a term denoting a part of, or a member of, the whole. For example, "tree" is a holonym of "bark," "trunk," and "limb."

> *Meronym* 部份: the opposite of holonymy; a word that names a part of a larger whole. For example, "finger" is a meronym of "hand" because a finger is part of a hand. Similarly "wheel" is a meronym of "automobile."

> *Metonymy* 转指: a figure of speech in which a concept is referred to by the name of something closely associated with that concept. For example, using *White House* instead of *President* is a use of metonymy.

> *Proposition*: refers to the meaning of a statement. For example, "All men are created equal" is a proposition.

6.2 FRAME, COLLOCATION, AND VERB VALENCY

Words by themselves are often insufficient to represent meanings without ambiguity. The theory of *frame semantics* developed by Filmore [1982] suggested that one could not understand the meaning of a word without access to all the essential knowledge related to that word. For example, one would not be able to understand the word *sell* without knowing all aspects of a commercial transaction. Thus, the word evokes a *frame* associated with *selling*, i.e., a structure of related concepts of semantic knowledge relating to the specific concept of selling.

A familiar example of the contextual nature of meanings is *collocation*. Collocation refers to the restrictions on how words can be used together either for semantic or pragmatic reasons. An example of collocation is the preposition–noun pair, which determines the appropriate prepositions for a particular noun; or the verb–object pair that determines which verbs and objects can be used together. The concept of Chinese collocation and methods for automatic Chinese collocation extraction will be explained in detail in Chapters 7 and 8, respectively.

How a word fits into the larger context can also have syntactic manifestations, in particular, in the case of verbs. The meaning of a verb determines whether it can take one, two, or three noun phrase arguments, known as *verb valency*. For example, the verb *to swim* can only take one argument, the verb *to buy* takes two arguments, and the verb *to present* can take up to three arguments. An argument has a semantic role to play with respect to the main verb in a clause. Semantic roles can be exemplified by the following:

> *Agent*: the semantic role of the animate entity that instigates or causes the happening denoted by the verb in the clause.

➤ *Patient*: the semantic role of an entity that is not the agent but is directly involved in or affected by the happening denoted by the verb in the clause.

➤ *Beneficiary*: the semantic role of the intended recipient who benefits from the happening denoted by the verb in the clause.

➤ *Instrument*: the semantic role of the entity (usually inanimate) that the agent uses to perform an action or start a process.

➤ *Recipient*: the semantic role of the animate entity that is passively involved in the happening denoted by the verb in the clause.

➤ *Locative*: the semantic role of the noun phrase that designates the place of the state or action denoted by the verb.

Semantic roles need to be distinguished from the syntactic notions of the subject and object. While a subject can be the agent, it need not be; it can also be the patient as in "the glass broke," where *the glass* is not the agent but the patient.

6.3   CHINESE DICTIONARIES/LEXICONS

Dictionaries, also known as lexicons, are important resources for NLP applications. Some word segmentation algorithms rely on quality electronic dictionaries. It is important therefore to understand special characteristics of Chinese dictionaries.

字典 *and* 词典. In English dictionaries, words are the basic units. But as the basic unit of Chinese writing is 字 (character), traditional Chinese dictionaries use characters rather than 词 (words) as the main unit. Modern dictionaries are, however, mostly word-based. Dictionaries that are character-based are referred to as 字典, while those that are word-based are known as 词典.

Organization of Chinese dictionaries. In addition to sound and meaning, by which entries in English dictionaries can be sorted, Chinese dictionaries can be organized by the graphic shape of characters as well, due to the rather indirect link between sound and shape in Chinese writing.

By sound. In dictionaries produced in mainland China, entries are ordered alphabetically using 拼音 *pinyin* with its 25 letters (the letter "v" is not used) in the same order as the English alphabet. Dictionaries produced in Taiwan may use 注音符号 *Zhùyīn fúhào instead*, which is more popularly known as *bopomofo* (after the names of the first four symbols in its alphabet) with its distinctively shaped symbols and own sequence of letters. A well-regarded dictionary of this kind, produced in mainland China, is 《现代汉语词典》 [Dictionary 2005].

A special dictionary that merits mention is the ABC Chinese–English Dictionary [DeFrancis et al. 2005], which uses strict alphabetical ordering of whole words instead of the more common alphabetic ordering of head characters in multi-character compounds. In the ABC dictionary, 仍 *réng* will be ordered before 认识 *rènshi* as the letter "g" precedes the letter "s." However, more often, it is the other way around since *réng* would be ordered after *rèn*. While the head character sort assumes prior breakdown of words into component characters, the ABC kind of dictionary does not.

In another kind of dictionary, words are sorted by sound; and it is called 倒序词典 (i.e., reverse-order dictionary), which sorts words by the last letter instead of the first. Even if rarer than the non-reverse kind, this kind of dictionary may nonetheless be useful for some applications, e.g., dictionary-based reverse maximum-matching word segmentation algorithm.

By graphic shape. As characters with unknown pronunciations cannot be looked up by sound, look-up methods using graphic shapes are introduced. All Chinese dictionaries have indices where characters are sorted by 部首, the graphic components known as radicals. One particular kind of graphic-based look-up method, which is not in common use anymore, is called 四角号码 (the Four Corner Method) which can uniquely identify a character by four strokes sampled at the four corners of a character.

By meaning. To cater for the requirements of writers, who may not know which words to use to express a particular meaning, there are also Chinese dictionaries with words organized by meaning categories, similar to Roget's Thesaurus for English. These dictionaries group synonyms or near synonyms in some structured categories. A particularly well-known Chinese dictionary of this kind is the 《同义词词林》 (CILIN) by Mei et al. [1983]. Its three-tiered meaning categories have provided much information about the relationship between words.

6.3.1   CILIN (《同义词词林》)

CILIN (《同义词词林》) is a contemporary Chinese thesaurus developed by a team of linguists for translation and writing purposes. Based on their semantic relationships, it classifies commonly used Chinese words in a hierarchical tree structure. The semantic knowledge contained in CILIN is useful to many NLP applications. Since Chinese is more semantically driven than other languages like English, it is very difficult for researchers to define a complete set of formal grammatical rules in spite of years of research efforts. Formulation of a Chinese sentence is determined more by the semantic relationship of the words rather than by their syntactical relationship. For this reason, knowledge about the semantic relationship of words is crucial to the understanding of natural language sentences in Chinese and is useful to many NLP applications such as WSD, IR, compound word detection, etc.

The CILIN contains approximately 63,600 entries for about 52,500 Chinese words, with each word having 1.2 entries on the average. It classifies the words according to a three-level semantic tree structure. This hierarchical structure reflects the semantic relationship between words and is defined by 12 major (top level), 95 medium (middle level), and 1,428 minor (bottom level) semantic classes. Each minor semantic class, in turn, consists of a set of words. Effectively, words under the same minor semantic class share the concept of this class. Figure 6.1 is an example from

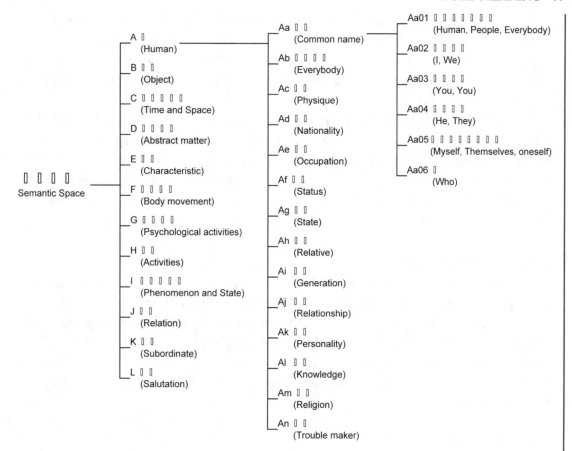

FIGURE 6.1: An example from 《同义词词林》.

the thesaurus. Referring to the figure, the hierarchical structure spans from left to right, i.e., A–L are the 12 major classes, Aa–An are examples of middle classes and Aa01–Aa06 are examples of minor classes. For example, the word 谁 (who), i.e., minor class Aa06, belongs to the middle class Aa [泛称 (common name)] and the major class A [人(human)]. Further, the minor class Aa06 [谁] consists of nine words as shown (p. 2, CILIN):

| 誰 | 孰 | 誰人 | 誰個 | 何人 | 何許人 | 哪人 | 哪位 | 若人 |

A word may appear in more than one branch of the hierarchy. On average, a word has 1.2 entries, i.e., 63K/52K. Further a major class covers multiple middle classes and each middle class may, in turn, have multiple minor classes. Two different words may have some overlapping in their semantic classes at different levels. The amount of overlapping in the semantic classes of two words reflects the similarity of the words.

The CILIN is a valuable knowledge source for Chinese NLP. Recently, Lua has studied the CILIN extensively. He proposed to use the conventional simple co-occurrence approach for extracting the semantic knowledge from the CILIN [Lua 1993]. However, simple co-occurrence statistics can only account for the strong relationships (i.e., a direct link) between the semantic classes in the CILIN and not their weak relationships (i.e., an indirect link). Wong et al. [1997] proposed an alternative approach which can extract partial semantic information from the CILIN.

6.4   WORDNETS

To meet the needs of NLP processing and semantic research, in general, a much enriched lexical network has been developed in the form of WordNets. Different from traditional dictionaries, WordNets explicitly show systematic relationships between the related entries, e.g., synonyms, antonyms, hyponyms, and hypernyms. The Princeton WordNet for English provided a model for WordNets for many other languages that followed [Miller et al. 1993; Felbaum 1999]. There are now two popular WordNets for Chinese, namely, the HowNet and CCD. They are introduced in the following sections.

6.4.1   HowNet

Overview. HowNet (http://www.keenage.com/) is an online extralinguistic common-sense knowledge system for the computation of meaning in human language technology (see also [Liu and Li 2002]). It unveils inter-concept relations and inter-attribute relations of concepts connoted in its Chinese–English lexicon. Compared with some existing linguistic knowledge resources, such as Roget's Thesaurus and WordNet, HowNet is unique in the following aspects:

1. The concept definition (DEF) in HowNet is based on sememes. Sememes are not written in natural language, but in a structured mark-up language. For example, the definition of 监狱 (prison) is DEF={InstitutePlace|场所:domain={police|警}, {detain|扣住: location={~}, patient={human|人:modifier={guilty|有罪}}}, {punish|处罚:location={~}, patient={human|人:modifier={guity|有罪}}}, which can be literally paraphrased as "A prison is an institutional place, which is the location where guilty people are detained and punished. The place belongs to the domain of police and law."

2. HowNet constructs a graph structure of its knowledge base on the inter-concept and inter-attribute relations. This is the fundamental difference between HowNet and other tree-

structure lexical databases. It reveals not only the concept relations within the same POS categories but also those across POS categories, especially the semantic role relations between nouns and verbs.

3. The representation is based on concepts denoted by words and expressions in both Chinese and English.

HowNet hypothesizes that all concepts can be reduced to the relevant sememes, and it defines a close set of sememes from which an open set of concepts can be composed. However, defining sememes is not easy. Broadly speaking, a sememe refers to the smallest basic semantic unit that cannot be reduced further. According to statistics, over 99% of the Chinese characters included in Xu Shen's etymological dictionary display some semantic information relevant to the real-word concepts that they denote. For example, sun (日) and moon (月) are relevant to nature, and father (父) and son (子) are relevant to human. Inspired by the aforesaid fact, sememes in HowNet are obtained by examining about 4,000 frequently used characters and their senses. This large-scale linguistic engineering process takes about 3 years of annotation and modification. At present, a set of 2,088 sememes exist in HowNet.

Sememes in HowNet are classified in a hierarchical structure, called taxonomy. Taxonomy mainly provides the hypernym–hyponym relations of concepts. HowNet organizes its sememes into the following four taxonomies: (1) taxonomy of events; (2) taxonomy of entity including things, parts, time, and space; (3) taxonomy of attributes; and (4) taxonomy of attribute–values. There are 805 event sememes, 152 entity sememes, 245 attribute sememes, and 886 attribute–value sememes. Figures 6.2 and 6.3 below illustrated the top levels of event hierarchy and entity hierarchy, respectively.

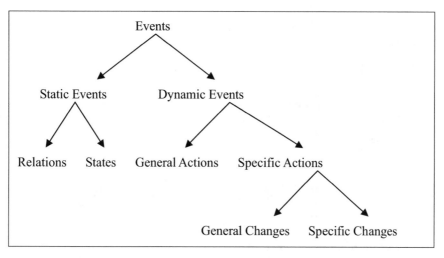

FIGURE 6.2: Top level of event hierarchy.

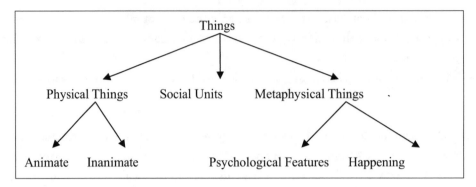

FIGURE 6.3: Top level of thing hierarchy.

Relations in HowNet. The meaning of concepts can be understood through relations. For example, we can understand the concept of "paper" through its relations with some other concepts, such as the concepts of "material," "write," "print," "wrap," etc., and the relations based on the attributes like form, use, texture, and so on. Relations are the soul of HowNet.

In terms of the depth that the computation of meaning reaches, the relations in HowNet can be classified into two types, namely, explicit and implicate relations. In general, explicit relations are established based on a single and relatively explicit sememe connection. There are 11 types of explicit relation in HowNet. They are (1) synonym, (2) synclass, (3) antonym, (4) converse, (5) hypernym, (6) hyponym, (7) part–whole, (8) value–attribute, (9) attribute–host, (10) cognate role-frame, and (11) semantic roles–event. Linguistically, the last four types are cross-POS relations. The relations among seven top-level sememes (namely, seven classes of sememes) are presented in Figure 6.4.

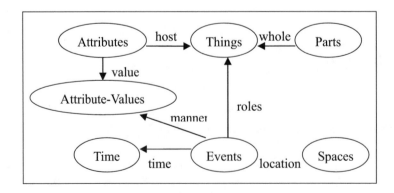

FIGURE 6.4: Relations of top-level sememes.

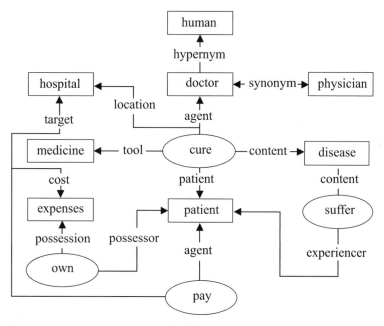

FIGURE 6.5: Concept relation of "doctor."

The relations can also be divided into two categories, namely, concept relation (CR) and attribute relation (AR). Figures 6.5 and 6.6 illustrate examples of concept relation net of "doctor" and attribute relation net of "paper."

While the explicit relations are directly represented by HowNet, the implicit relations need to be computed from it. Currently, HowNet represents mainly two kinds of implicit relations, i.e., the relation of concept relevance and of concept similarity.

HowNet is designed for NLP applications, which are computational in nature. It is practically a system by the computer, for the computer, and, expectantly, of the computer. Using HowNet, concept relevance and concept similarity can be computed [Liu and Li 2002]. Concept relevance measures how concepts are related in multiple-sememe connections, and concept similarity measures the similarity between any senses of any concepts in the HowNet. For instance, "doctor" and "dentist" are of high similarity, but "doctor" and "fever" are of very low similarity although they are of high relevance.

6.4.2   Chinese Concept Dictionary

The CCD is a WordNet-like lexicon of contemporary Chinese developed by the Institution of Computational Linguistics, Peking University, China [Yu et al. 2001a; Liu et al. 2002, 2003]. It

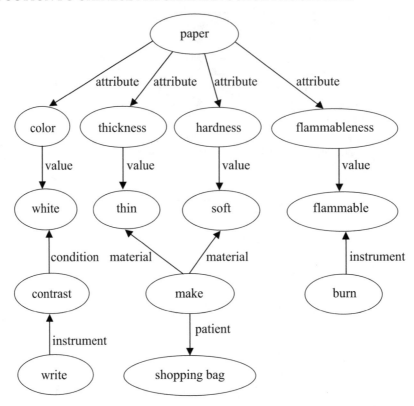

FIGURE 6.6: Attribute relation of "paper."

is a bilingual Chinese–English WordNet following the framework of WordNet. It is compatible with WordNet structurally because such concept-to-concept relations are defined using synsets. CCD records synonyms, antonyms, hypernyms–hyponyms, meronyms–holonyms, and collocations of words as well as their major POS information including nouns, verbs, adjectives, and adverbs. In the CCD, the characteristics of Chinese are highlighted by not only encoding the lexical content of Chinese but also bringing out the relationships between the content and the concept.

Overview. The CCD was designed to provide linguistic knowledge to support Chinese syntactic and semantic analyses.

There are three major characteristics in CCD, which make it distinct from WordNet. First, nouns in CCD include words of time [e.g., 下午 (afternoon)]; location [e.g., 西部 (Western)]; direction/position [e.g., 上 (up)]; numerals [e.g., 甲 (first)]; quantifiers [e.g., 批 (lots)]; also some pronouns; differentiation [e.g., 金/银 (gold/silver), 男/女 (male/female)]; suffixes [e.g.性 (gender), 器 (apparatus), 仪 (protocols), 机 (machines)]; idioms (e.g., 八拜之交, 铜墙铁壁); semi-idioms (木头疙瘩、光杆司令); and abbreviated forms (政协). Despite the subcategorization, we simply refer them as nouns, in general. Moreover, the intension and extension of verbs, adjectives, and adverbs in CCD are different from those in WordNet. A concept is represented by a set of synonyms with the same POS in WordNet. But semantically, concepts from different POS may be related in some way. For instance, 战争 (battle) and 打仗 (fighting in a war) [or 战斗 (fight)] are associated although the first one is a noun and the second is a verb in Chinese. CCD alleviates this restriction in WordNet. An attribute of association is appended to the feature structure of a concept. Second, the relations described in CCD are much finer than WordNet. For example, synonyms relation is divided into equivalence and similarity, antonyms relation is divided into essential antonyms and nonessential ones, three new types of meronyms–holonyms relations are introduced in CCD. Finally, examples of collocations are selected from real corpora with quantitative descriptions. It is a useful extension of WordNet.

Structurally, following the framework of WordNet, CCD distinguishes between nouns, verbs, adjectives, and adverbs. Every synset contains a group of synonymous words or collocations and defines a concept. Different senses of a word are in different synsets. The meaning of the synsets is further clarified with short-defining glosses (i.e., definitions and/or example sentences). Most synsets are connected to other synsets via a number of semantic relations. These relations vary based on the type of word. The most important relations maintained in CCD are listed in Table 6.1.

In these relationships, many of them are reflective and are listed in Table 6.2.

Nouns in CCD. The first problem is to decide what the primitive semantic components should be. One important criterion is that, collectively, they should accommodate every Chinese noun. To be compatible with WordNet, CCD adopted 25 unique primitive elements that are listed in Table 6.3. These hierarchies vary widely in size and are not mutually exclusive; some cross-referencing is required, but on the whole, they cover distinct conceptual and lexical domains.

In principle, there is no limit to the number of levels an inheritance system can have. Lexical inheritance systems, however, seldom go more than 10 levels deep, and the deepest examples usually contained are technical terminology. In the initial semantic units of nouns in CCD, some mother

TABLE 6.1: Relations in CCD							
RELATIONS	LABEL	RELATIONS	LABEL	RELATIONS	LABEL	RELATIONS	LABEL
Antonym	!	Antonym	!	Antonym	!	Antonym	!
Hyponym	□	Troponym	□	Similar	&	Derived from	\
Hypernym	@	Hypernym	@	Relational Adj.	\		
Meronym	#	Entailment	*	Also See	^		
Holonym	%	Cause	>	Attribute	□		
Attribute	□	Also See	^				

TABLE 6.2: The reflective relation pointers in CCD

POINTER	REFLECT
Antonym	Antonym
Hyponym	Hypernym
Hypernym	Hyponym
Holonym	Meronym
Meronym	Holonym
Similar to	Similar to
Attribute	Attribute

node for concepts is defined. For instance, *animal, human being*, and *plant* are categorized as *organism*, while *organism* and *object* could be organized by *entity*. In this way, the 25 initial semantic units are structured in 11 basic categories as follows (see Figure 6.7).

In CCD, the relations between noun concepts include synonymy, antonymy, hyponymy, meronymy, and attribute.

(a) Synonymy

Synonyms are different words with identical or very similar meanings. Words that are synonyms are said to be synonymous, and the state of being a synonym is called synonymy. According to the definition by Leibniz, two expressions are synonymous if the substitution of one for the other never changes the truth value of a sentence in which the substitution is made. By that definition,

TABLE 6.3: The primitive semantic units of nouns in CCD

{act, action, activity}	{ animal, fauna}	{artifact}	{attribute, property}	{body, corpus}
{cognition, knowledge}	{communication}	{event, happening}	{feeling, emotion}	{food}
{group, collection}	{location, place}	{motive}	{natural object}	{natural phenomenon}
{ person, human being}	{plant, flora}	{possession}	{process}	{quantity, amount}
{relation}	{shape}	{state, condition}	{substance}	{time}

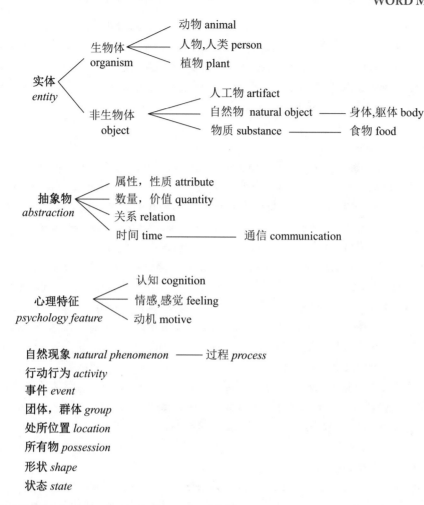

FIGURE 6.7: The basic categories of nouns in CCD.

true synonyms are rare. A weaker version of this definition would make synonymy relative to a context; that is, two expressions are synonymous in a linguistic context *C* if the substitution of one for the other in *C* does not alter the truth value. Note that if concepts are represented by synsets, and synonyms must be interchangeable, the words in different syntactic categories cannot be synonyms (cannot form synsets) because they are not interchangeable. For example, 计算机 and 电脑 (computer) could be changed in almost all contexts *C* without changing the semantics of *C*. Thus, they are synonyms.

CCD further enriches the contents of nouns by recording the following information of the nouns. First, CCD records the word formation rule of the nouns if applicable: attribute+part+noun noun. For example, 长 (long) is an attribute of a noun 鹿 (deer), and 颈 (neck) is a part of 鹿 (deer); their combination forms a new noun 长颈鹿 (giraffe). Second, CCD records the syntactic relations between the morphemes forming a noun. For example, 美人 (beautiful girl) has two morphemes 美 (beautiful) and 人 (person). Third, the refined noun categorization information are recorded. The refined categorization information includes abbreviations [北大 vs. 北京大学 (Peking University)], regular and irregular words (教师 vs. 孩子王, both meaning teacher), and sentiment polarity (教师 neutral vs. 臭老九 negative, both meaning teacher).

(b)　Antonymy

Antonyms are words that lie in an inherently incompatible binary relationship as in the opposite pairs. The notion of incompatibility here means that one word in an opposite pair entails that it is not the other pair member. Antonymy is a lexical relation between word forms, not a semantic relation between word meanings. The antonym relation is symmetric. Here are some examples of antonyms in CCD: 加 (add) vs. 减 (minus), 国王 (king) vs. 王后 (queen), and 儿子 (son) vs. 女儿 (daughter). Note that the antonym relations are always valid under specific condition. The notation of antonym in CCD is divided into essential and nonessential in some relationship. Essential antonym is named for words A and B on one specific condition: A is the only antonym choice. For instance, 丈夫 (husband)–妻子(wife) is essential antonym in the relationship of husband–wife; that is, under the relationship of husband–wife, "x is not a husband" is equal to "x is wife." On the other hand, nonessential antonyms are named for words A and B on one specific condition: A is not the only antonym choice. For instance, under the relationship of persons with ages, 老人 (elder) and 孩子 (children) as well as 老人 (elder) and 年轻人 (young man) are two nonessential antonyms. The anonym knowledge recorded in 现代汉语规范用法大辞典 and 反义词词典 are adopted in CCD.

(c)　Hyponymy–Hypermymy

Unlike synonymy and antonymy, which are lexical relations between word forms, hyponymy–hypernymy is a semantic relation between word meanings. If the proposition "X is a kind of Y" is true, then X is the hyponym of Y (or Y is the hypernym of Y). Hyponymy is transitive and asymmetrical, and, since there is normally a single superordinate, it generates a hierarchical semantic structure, in which a hyponym is said to be below its superordinate. Such hierarchical representations are widely used in the construction of IR systems, where they are called inheritance systems: a hyponym inherits all the features of the more generic concept and adds at least one feature that distinguishes it from its superordinate and from any other hyponyms of that superordinate. An example of hierarchical hyponymy is given below.

树 (tree)
　　　　=>木本植物 (woody plant)
　　　　=>维管植物 (vascular plan)
　　　=>植物，植物生命体 (plant)

=>生命形式，生物体，生物 (life form)

=>实体 (entity)

(d) Meronymy

The part–whole relation between nouns is generally considered to be a semantic relation, called meronymy. It has an inverse relationship: if X is a meronym of Y, then X is said to be a holonym of Y. Meronyms are distinguishing features that hyponyms can inherit. Consequently, meronymy and hyponymy become intertwined in complex ways. For example, if 喙 (beak) and 翼 (wing) are meronyms of 鸟 (bird), and if 燕子 (swallow) is a hyponym of 鸟, then, by inheritance, 喙 (beak) and 翼 (wing) must also be meronyms of 燕子 (swallow). The "part of" relation is often compared to the "kind of" relation: both are asymmetric and (with reservations) transitive and can relate terms hierarchically. That is to say, parts can have parts: 手指 (finger) is a part of 手 (hand), 手 (hand) is a part of 胳膊 (arm), and 胳膊 (arm) is a part of 身体 (body) (i.e., 手指 is a meronym of 手, 手 is a meronym of 胳膊, and 胳膊 is a meronym of 身体). But the "part of" test is not always a reliable test of meronymy. A basic problem with meronymy is that people will accept the test frame, "X is a part of Y" for a variety of part–whole relations. There are six types of meronymy in CCD. The first three types as follows are compatible with WordNet:

1. $w\#p\rightarrow w'$ indicates that individual w is a component part of individual w' [e.g., 车轮 (wheel)–车 (car)].

2. $w\#m\rightarrow w'$ indicate that w is a member of set (composed by individual w') [e.g., 树 (tree)–森林 (forest)].

3. $w\#s\rightarrow w'$ indicates that w is the stuff that w' is made from [e.g., 钢 (steel)–钢板 (armor plate)].

In addition, three other types of meronymy are introduced in CCD as follows:

1. $w\#a\rightarrow w'$ indicates that w is a subarea of w' [e.g., 石家庄 (Shijiazhuang City)–河北 (Hebei Province)].

2. $w\#e\rightarrow w'$ indicates that event w is a part of event w' [e.g., 开幕式 (opening)–会议 (conference)].

3. $w\#t\rightarrow w'$ indicates that time w is a part of time w' [e.g., 唐朝 (Tang Dynasty)–古代 (ancient time)].

(e) Attribute

CCD includes attribute components. Feature structures are the nodes in CCD to distinguish a concept from its sister concepts. For instance, 燕子 (swallow)@→候鸟

(migratory), the feature structure to distinguish 燕子 (swallow) and 天鹅 (swan) is described in Table 6.4:

where: attribute is a set of descriptions, usually adjectives; part is a set of main parts distinct from those of sister node concepts, usually nouns; function is a set of main functions distinct from those of sister node concepts, usually verbs, i.e., the verbs with the noun as one of the arguments; and association is a set of verbs describing an event such as the association of 车祸 (traffic accident) is 撞车 (collision).

Verbs in CCD. There are 15 basic semantic categories for verbs in CCD that are compatible with WordNet as follows:

1. 身体动作动词 (verbs of bodily care and functions)
2. 变化动词 (verbs of change)
3. 通信动词 (verbs of communication)
4. 竞争动词 (competition verbs)
5. 消费动词 (consumption verbs)
6. 接触动词 (contact verbs)
7. 认知心理动词 (cognition verbs)
8. 创造动词 (creation verbs)
9. 运动动词 (motion verbs)
10. 情感心理动词 (emotion or psych verbs)
11. 状态动词 (stative verbs)
12. 感知动词 (perception verbs)
13. 领属动词 (verbs of possession)
14. 社会交互 (verbs of social interaction)
15. 气象动词 (weather verbs)

In CCD, the relations between verbal concepts include synonymy, antonymy, hyponymy, entailment, causal relation, and sentence frame.

TABLE 6.4: The feature structures of nous in CCD	
ATTRIBUTE	黑 (BLACK)
Part	
Function	报春 (Heralding Spring)
Association	

(a) Synonymy

Two verbs are truly synonymous if and only if they can substitute each other in all contexts. In Chinese, few verbs are strict synonyms. If two verbs, $\bar{U}$ and $\hat{U}$, could substitute each other in almost all contexts, they are defined as equivalent synonyms. If they can substitute in some contexts (not all), they are named near synonyms. Both equivalent and near synonyms are considered synonyms in CCD. Note that the syntactic properties of two synonyms must be identical [e.g., {死, 逝世, 去世, 升天, . . .} are all representing dead].

Similar to nouns, CCD also provides the abbreviation information, regular/irregular use, and sentiment polarity of verbs. For instance, in the synset {死, 亡, 死亡, 去世, 逝世, 过世, 仙逝, 老, 归西, 上西天, 完蛋, 一命呜呼, and 见阎王, which all mean dead}, 死 去世 逝世 are regular verbs labeled r and 过世 老 归西 上西天 are irregular verbs labeled i. Meanwhile, 死 亡 死亡 are labeled neutral, 去世 逝世 过世 老 仙逝 are positive, and 完蛋 一 命呜呼 见阎王 are negative.

(b) Antonymy

Compared to nouns, the semantics of a verb is more difficult to describe: it seems impossible to distinguish the antonymy relationship between two given verbs in the way of nouns. Much real-world knowledge is needed for this purpose. For instance, both 来 (come)/ 去 (go) [or 升 (rise)/降 (descend)] and问 (ask)/告诉 (inform) exhibit antonymy relations for different reasons, namely, the direction of movement of agent for 来 (come)/去(go) [or 升 (rise)/降 (descend)] and the direction of information for 问 (ask)/告诉 (inform).

The determination of antonymy relation for verbs in CCD is based on 现代汉语规范用法 大辞典 [Zhou 1997].

Furthermore, some verbal antonyms can be formed from morphological processes. For example, in Chinese, nouns 规范 (standard) and 形式 (formality) can be transformed to verb 规范化 (standardize) and 形式化 (formularize) by adding a verbal morpheme 化. Naturally, the antonym information recorded in 规范 (standard) and 形式 (form) can be used to obtain the verb antonyms, i.e., 非规范化 (non-standardize) and 非形式化 (deformularize).

(c) Hypernymy

In CCD, $\bar{U}$ is a hypernym of $\hat{U}$ if and only if the proposition "to $\hat{U}$ is to $\bar{U}$ in some particular manner" is true. Hyponym $\hat{U}$ entails its hypernymy $\bar{U}$, or $\bar{U}$ takes place of $\hat{U}$ without changing the truth value of the sentence, which is similar to the hyponymy–hypernymy relation for nouns in CCD. Hyponymy relation is a special kind entailment relation, but the converse is not true. For example, 打鼾 (snore) entails 睡觉 (sleep), but the former is not the hyponymy verb of the latter.

(d) Entailment

In logic, *entailment* describes a relation between propositions: a proposition *P* entails another proposition *Q* if and only if there is no truth assignment such that *P* is true while *Q* is false. Thus, entailment is a kind of semantic relationship describing truth relation between *P* and *Q*. CCD records the following four entailment cases between verbs:

1. The temporal interval (or point) of verb $\bar{U}$ embeds in that of $\acute{U}$. For instance, 打鼾 (snore) entails 睡觉 (sleep). Entailment relation between verbs is much like the meronymy relation between nouns.

2. The temporal interval (or point) of verb $\bar{U}$ is equal to that of $\acute{U}$. For instance, 跛行 (limp) entails 行走 (walk) because 跛行 (limp) is a special kind of 行走 (walk).

3. The temporal interval of verb $\bar{U}$ has nothing to do with that of $\acute{U}$. But inferring back from $\bar{U}$, we could get $\acute{U}$. Or, if $\acute{U}$ does not happen, neither does $\bar{U}$. For instance, 成功 (succeed) entails 尝试 (try), as one would never succeed (i.e., 成功) without trying (i.e., 尝试).

4. The temporal interval of verb $\bar{U}$ has nothing to do with that of $\acute{U}$. But inferring back from $\bar{U}$, we could get $\acute{U}$. For instance, 给 (give) entails 拥有 (own) such that a person A 给 (give) another person B something X results in B owns (拥有) X instead of A.

The tree in Figure 6.8 shows four cases of entailment.

In WordNet, both part–meronymy relation and backward presupposition are named entailment, which is a shortcoming of WordNet. CCD distinguishes the entailment into four cases.

(e) Causal relation

The causative relation picks out two verb concepts, one causative [e.g., 给 (give)], the other might be called the "resultative" (e.g., 拥有 own). Similar to other entailment relation, causal relation is unidirectional. There is a very special case in causal relations: if *x* causes *y*, then *x* entails *y* [e.g., 驱逐 (expel) and 离开 (leave), 馈赠 (donate) and 拥有 (own)].

(f) Sentence frame

A sentence frame describes the arguments of verbs. For instance, the sentence frame of concept {吃, 啃, 叼, . . .} is <生物体, 生物体>, which describes the semantic roles of agent and patient, respectively. The valence of {吃, 啃, 叼, …} is then 2. The principle of substitution permits us to identify the semantic class of arguments (Table 6.5).

Adjectives in CCD. A descriptive adjective describes some attributes of noun such as 大, 小, 高, 低, 重, etc. Chinese adjectives are quite different from their English counterparts; for ex-

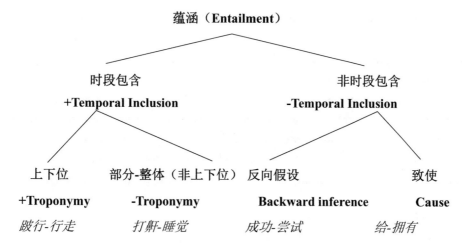

FIGURE 6.8: Cases of entailment in CCD.

TABLE 6.5: The semantic roles in CCD

AGN agent 施事	COS course 经事
ESS essive 当事	GOL goal 向事
EXP experience 感事	SCP scope 范围
GEN genitive 领事	RSN reason 缘由
PAT patient 受事	INT intention 意图
IMP impelled 致事	TIM time 时间
RST result 结果	SPA space 空间
CON content 内容	MAN manner 方式
BRL belongings 属事	INS instrument 工具
PAR part 分事	MAT material 材料
CAT category 类事	QNT quantity 数量
COM comitative 涉事	DUR duration 历时
SOR source 源事	FRQ frequency 频次

ample, in 音乐器材 (musical instrument), 音乐 (music) is a noun, but it serves as an adjective here. In WordNet, relational adjectives are only at attributive position, similar to a noun semantically (e.g., musical instrument and musical child). The former is descriptive, while the latter is relational. However, there is no relational adjective in Chinese.

CCD classifies Chinese adjectives into common and special adjectives as shown in Table 6.6.

This classification represents the main characteristic of Chinese adjectives: common adjectives are scalar (i.e., corresponding adjectives in English have comparative degrees), while the special ones are polar. Special adjectives could be described by feature structures or other discrete methods. WordNet does not partition English adjectives in this way; thus, CCD particularly emphasizes syntactic–semantic differences.

(a) Synonymy

A synset of adjectives is a set of adjectives. Adjectives that can be substituted in all contexts are deemed to exhibit adjectival synonymy. For instance, since 干燥, 干枯, 干爽 are the similar adjectives of 干 (dry), {干, 干燥, 干枯, 干爽} forms an adjectival synset.

(b) Similarity

If a set of adjective concept, $c_1, c_2, \ldots c_n$ are similar to a adjective concept c, then they form an earth satellite-like structure (see Figure 6.9). Let us say c is a central concept and $c_1, c_2, \ldots c_n$ are satellite concepts. There is only one central adjective in a synset, to which the other adjectives around it are similar [e.g., 干 and 干燥 (dry)]. The relationship between

TABLE 6.6: Classification of adjectives in CCD

COMMON ADJECTIVES CAN BE MODIFIED BY 很 (VERY)		SPECIAL ADJECTIVES CANNOT BE MODIFIED BY 很 (VERY)		
		Serve as adverbial modifier	Not serve as adverbial modifier	
大				
小		高速	Serve as attribute	Not serve as attribute
高		大规模	男	红彤彤
低		小范围	女	绿油油
重				

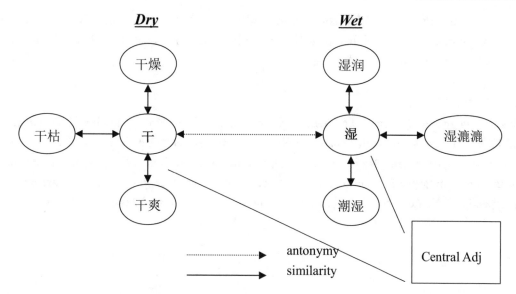

FIGURE 6.9: Adjectives in CCD.

central concepts and satellite concepts are directly similar (e.g., 干 and 干燥), while the ones between non-central concepts are indirectly similar (e.g., 干燥 and 干爽).

(c)   Antonymy

The basic relation between adjectives is directly antonymous such as 干 (dry) and 湿 (wet) shown above. The antonymous relation between non-central concepts is termed indirect antonyms [e.g., 干爽 (dry) and 湿漉漉 (wet)].

Adverbs in CCD. Adverbs in English are normally derived from adjectives. Their synonyms and antonyms are inherited from their corresponding adjectives where a pointer in WordNet links adverbs and their corresponding adjectives. However, such a linkage does not exist in Chinese. Thus, no such pointers are used in CCD. CCD maintains two kinds of relations as follows:

(a)   Synonymy: Two adverbs are synonymous if they can substitute one another in all contexts. For example, 突然 and 忽然 both means suddenly.

(b)   Antonymy: Two adverbs are antonymous if their substitution alters the contextualized meaning or logical truth. Adverbial antonymy is rare in Chinese.

Status of CCD. CCD version 1.0 contains synsets and relations of about 66,000 noun concepts, 12,000 verbal concepts, and 21,000 adjectival and adverbial concepts. The annotated concepts can be aligned with about 100,000 concepts in English WordNet version 1.6. It plays an important role in the construction of Global WordNet. More information related to CCD can be found at http://icl.pku.edu.cn/icl_groups/ccd.asp.

6.5   SUMMARY

This chapter gives an overview of three major Chinese linguistic resources, namely CILIN, HowNet, and CCD. These resources are valuable to NLP applications, such as concept-based IR, information extraction, document classification, WSD, and machine translation. In addition, other similar resources including printed dictionaries, electronic lexicons, corpora, transcripts, etc., are outlined in Appendix A. Some of these resources are openly available from the Internet.

·   ·   ·   ·   ·

CHAPTER 7

Chinese Collocations

Collocation is a lexical phenomenon where two or more words are habitually combined together as some conventional way of saying things. For example, in Chinese, 历史/n 包袱/n (historical burden) rather than 历史/n 行李/n (historical luggage) is said, even though 包袱/n (baggage) and 行李/n (luggage) are synonymous. However, no one can explain why 历史 (historical) must collocate with 包袱 (burden). Therefore, collocations are closely knit and frequently used word combinations. The collocated words always have syntactic or semantic relations, but they cannot be accounted for directly by general syntactic or semantic rules. They mainly reflect the conventional nature of natural language. Collocation can bring out different meanings a word can carry, and it plays an indispensable role in expressing the most appropriate meaning in a given context. Consequently, collocation knowledge is widely employed in many NLP tasks such as in Word Sense Disambiguation [Church 1988; Sinclair 1991], Machine Translation [Gitska et al. 2000], Information Retrieval [Mitra et al. 1997], and Natural Language Generation [Smadja 1993].

7.1 CONCEPT OF COLLOCATION

7.1.1 Definitions

Collocations are commonly found in natural language expressions. Although they are easily comprehensible by most readers, a precise definition of collocation remains elusive [Manning and Schütze 1999]. Various definitions have been proposed depending on different collocation features.

The terms collocation and collocability were first introduced by Firth [1957]. Firth did not really give an explicit definition of collocation. He illustrated the notion by examples. Firth emphasized the concept of company of words. He argued that words in natural languages are not individually used rather they always accompanied by other words. Moreover, collocation is not only a juxtaposition of words but also an order of mutual expectancy. That is, the words in a collocation have customary or habitual places and are mutually expected and comprehended. Firth's concept of collocation emphasized the co-occurrence of words, and meaning relations between words.

Halliday [1976] gave a definition of collocation under the framework of lexis and suggested that collocation was the syntagmatic relation of linear co-occurrence together with some measure of significant proximity, either with a scale or at least by a cutoff point. In Halliday's definition, linear co-occurrence is fundamental and is, in fact, the only discriminative criterion. Syntactic dependency or relations are not considered.

Halliday's definition was adopted by Sinclair [1991] in his book, *Corpus, Concordance, Collocation*. Sinclair pointed out that words were used in pairs or groups, and language users were considered to have available to them "a large number of semi-pre-constructed phrases that constitute single choices." Sinclair regarded all frequently co-occurring words as the collocations of a word, even those words that have no direct syntactic or semantic relation. Both Halliday and Sinclair regarded collocated words (lexical items) as mutual predications and mutual attractions.

Some linguists argued that collocation study should not only be based on Halliday's item-oriented approach but also on an integrated approach. Greenbaum [1974] proposed to integrate both local syntactic structure and sentence patterns into collocation study. Through studies of the collocations between verbs and their intensifiers, Greenbaum pointed out that an integrated approach, which singled out the collocation behavior of a clearly delimited syntactic configuration, could yield the best results. Mitchell [1975] further proposed to integrate grammatical generalizations, meanings, and grammatical functions in collocation study. The *Oxford Dictionary of Current Idiomatic English* [Cowie and Mackin 1975] is a collocation dictionary following this integrated approach. In this dictionary, a collocation is defined as the co-occurrence of two or more lexical items as realizations of structural elements within a given syntactic pattern [Cowie 1978]. It specifies that co-occurring lexical items must be within the predefined syntactic patterns.

Kjellmer [1984] defined collocations as lexically determined and grammatically restricted sequences of words. Only the co-occurred words have both co-occurrence significance, and well-formed grammar are regarded as collocations.

Benson [1985] defined collocations as recurrent, fixed, identifiable, nonidiomatic phrases and constructions. Benson categorized collocations into grammatical and lexical collocations. A grammatical collocation is defined as a phrase consisting of a dominant word plus a particle. Typical grammatical collocations include verb+preposition (abide by, account for), noun+preposition (access to), and adjective+preposition (absent from). A lexical collocation is a combination of nouns, adjectives, verbs, and adverbs, but it does not include prepositions, infinitives, or clauses. The categorization of Benson et al. [1986] guided the compilation of the *BBI Combinatory Dictionary of English*. In Benson's collocation framework, grammatical restrictions dominate. Recurrent co-occurrence is not an essential feature for a collocation. Later, Benson [1990] generalized the notion of collocation to an arbitrary and recurrent word combination. This definition is adopted by many computational linguists [Smadja 1993; Sun et al. 1997].

Furthermore, semantic restrictions within collocations are studied. Carter [1987] pointed out that syntactic and semantic statements were often essential in studying collocations. Some researchers proposed that collocations should only be word combinations whose whole meanings could not be predicted from their components. There are other researchers who thought that such a restriction was too strict and hence would be impractical [Allerton 1984].

In corpus linguistics, collocation is defined (see Wikipedia) as a sequence of words or terms which co-occur more often than would be expected by chance. Some researchers emphasize the habitual and recurrent use of collocations [Gistak 2000]. Similarly, Manning and Schütze [1999] stated that "a collocation is an expression consisting of two or more words that correspond to some conventional way of saying things." It is clear that many corpus linguistic researchers are engaged in the identification and study of habitual use of lexical items which is also applicable to NLP research.

More discussions on the definition of collocation in the field of linguistics can be found in *The Definition and Research System of the Word Collocation* [Wei 2002].

7.1.2 Collocations in Chinese

Generally speaking, the definition of Chinese collocations is similar to English collocations. There are, however, three major differences between them.

1. Chinese sentences are written in continuous character strings rather than discrete words. Thus, segmentation of character strings into words is the first step in processing. Due to different segmentation results, some collocations like 高/a 质量/n may be processed as one word instead of two. That is to say, Chinese collocation is based on word segmentation results.

2. The use of Chinese words is more flexible, i.e., the same word form may have more than one part of speech. For example, a word 安全 have three parts of speech, i.e., a noun meaning "safety," an adjective meaning "safe," and an adverb meaning "safely." The collocations corresponding to different parts of speech always have different characteristics. For example, when a noun 安全/n collocates with a verb 生产/v (safety in manufacturing), 安全/n always occurs following 生产/v while an adverb 安全/ad always occurs before 生产/v (manufacture safely). Therefore, Chinese collocation research should be based on the word form plus its part of speech; that is, 安全/n and 安全/ad are regarded as two different words and their collocations should be studied separately.

3. The study of Chinese collocation, especially for NLP purposes, focuses on the collocations between content words, i.e., noun, verb, adjective, adverb, determiner, directional word, and nominalized verbs [Zhang et al. 1992]. Collocations related to noncontent words, such as prepositions, are not a major issue. The grammatically associated word combinations, such as 吃-着 (eating) and 在-路上 (on the way), are never considered as collocations.

In this and the following chapter (i.e., Chapter 8), the definition of Chinese collocation, given by Xu et al. [2006] is adopted. The definition was designed for NLP purposes and is stated as follows:

> *A **collocation** is a recurrent and conventional expression containing two or more content word combinations that hold syntactic and/or semantic relations.*

In other words, the study of Chinese collocation in this book focuses on the lexically restricted word combinations in Chinese with emphasis on semantically and syntactically collocated word combinations such as 浓/a 茶/n (strong tea) 热烈/ad 欢迎/v (warm welcome). The grammatically associated word combinations, such as 吃/v-着/u (eating) and 在/r 路上/n (on the way), are not considered collocations.

From another perspective, based on the number of components, collocations are divided into *bigram collocation*, which contains two words like 热烈/ad 欢迎/v, and *n-gram collocation*, which contains more than two words such as 祖国/n 统一/vn 大业/n (reunification of the motherland). The co-occurrence of two or more collocated words can appear sequentially, referred to as *uninterrupted collocation*, or be separated by other words in between, referred to as *interrupted collocation*.

7.2 QUALITATIVE PROPERTIES

From a linguistic viewpoint, collocations are different from free word combinations at one extreme and idioms at the other [Mckeown et al. 2000]. There are a number of qualitative properties which are applicable to Chinese as follows:

1. Collocations are recurrent co-occurrences. As rightfully pointed out by Hoey [1991], "collocation has long been the name given to the relationship a lexical item has with items that appear with greater than random probability in its context." This means that collocations occur frequently in similar context and they always appear in certain fixed patterns. This is the most important property of a collocation differing from a random words combination.

2. Collocations are of habitual use [Smadja 1993]. Many collocations cannot be described by general syntactic or semantic rules. For instance, we only say 浓/a 茶/n (strong tea), but not 烈/a 茶/n (powerful tea). The choice of which to use is completely habitual. No syntax or semantic reason can explain the particular choice of words.

3. Collocations are to limited extent compositional [Manning and Schütze 1999; Xu et al. 2006]. Brundage et al. [1992] introduced the term "compositional" to describe the property where the meaning of an expression could be predicted from the meaning of its compo-

nents. Free word combinations can be generated by linguistic rules and their meanings are the combinations of their components. At the other extreme, idioms are always noncompositional, implying that their meanings are different from the combinations of their components. For example, the literal meaning of a Chinese idiom 缘木求鱼 is to climb a tree to catch fish; however, the real meaning of this collocation is a fruitless approach. Collocations are in between free combinations and idioms. They are expected to be compositional to a limited extent. In other words, collocations are expected to have additional meanings beyond their literal meaning. On the other hand, for those word combinations that have little additional meaning over the literal meaning, they can also be regarded as collocations if they show close semantic restrictions between their components.

4. Collocations are substitutable and modifiable only to a limited extent. Limited substitution here refers to the fact that a word within a collocation cannot be replaced freely by other words in a context, even its synonyms. For example, 包袱/n (baggage) and 行李/n (luggage) have very similar meanings in Chinese. However, when they collocate with 历史/n (historical), we only say 历史/n 包袱/n to mean historical burden but never 历史/n 行李/n. Also, collocations cannot be modified freely by adding modifiers or through grammatical transformations. For example, a collocation of 斗志/n 昂扬/a (high spirit) does not allow further modification or insertion of materials between the two parts.

5. Most collocations are grammatically well formed. Especially, most bigram collocations have direct syntactic relation or dependency, except for the idiomatic ones. Therefore, collocations always have both syntactic and semantic relations. Meanwhile, many collocations have fixed linear order. For example, in verb–object Chinese collocations, the verb always appears before object. That is 弹/v 钢琴/n and 踢/v 足球/n are correct collocations, while 钢琴/n 弹/v and 足球/n 踢/v are wrong.

6. Collocations are domain dependent. The collocations frequently used in one domain may be seldom used in another domain, especially the technical collocations. For example, 专家/n 系统/n means expert system, which is frequently used in computer science, but it seldom appears, in general. Meanwhile, some collocations are more frequently used in oral, while some are always used in formal text. It means that collocations are domain-dependent.

7. Collocations are language-dependent, which means that some collocations in one language are no longer collocations when translated to another language (e.g., when a Chinese collocation 开/v 枪/n is translated to a single word fire in English). Meanwhile, many collocations cannot be translated simply into word for word such as play ball as 打/v 球/n and play piano as 弹/v 钢琴/n. This can be attributed to the conventional patterns used in different languages.

7.3   QUANTITATIVE FEATURES

Based on the qualitative properties above, several computational quantitative features are defined, which can be used to estimate the strength of the association between words. This is, in fact, a means to realize the concept of collocability previously introduced by Firth [1957].

1. Corresponding to the recurrent property, quantitative features based on co-occurrence frequency can be used to estimate the co-occurrence significance of all collocation candidates. The ones having higher significance are always true collocations. Different statistical metric and extraction strategies have been employed such as absolute and relative co-occurrence frequency [Choueka 1983; Choueka 1988], pointwise mutual information [Church 1990; Sun et al. 1997]), Z-score mean and variance [Rogghe 1973; Smadja 1993], t-test [Yu et al. 2003b], χ^2-test [Manning and Schütze 1999], and likelihood ratio test [Dunning 1993; Zhou et al. 2001; Lü et al. 2004]. More details on these features will be presented in Chapter 8.2.1.

2. Collocations are of conventional nature. On one hand, the words are used in combination which leads to strong co-occurrence. On the other hand, the context of collocations normally shows high homogeneity. It means that information of its context are helpful for estimating the association strength of the collocation. Features based on the entropy and mutual information of context have been used for estimating association of collocation [Zhai 1997]. More discussions on these features will be presented in Chapter 8.2.3.

3. Collocations are only to a limited extent compositional. Because the compositionality of word combinations is hard to be directly estimated by computer systems, few computational features corresponding to compositionality were proposed. The translation test is one method to estimate the compositionality of a collocation [Manning and Schütze 1999]. If the translation result of a word combination is different from the combination of the translations of its individual component words combined, this combination is a true collocation.

4. Collocations have limited substitutability and limited modifiability. Synonymy substitution ratio is an effective feature for estimating substitutability within a bigram combination. For a bigram, there are two corresponding synonym sets for each observing word. If the bigram pair of one observing word and one synonym of another observing word frequently co-occur in the corpus above a certain threshold, the second observing word is regarded substitutable by its synonym. A smaller value of synonym substitution ratio means this word combination tends to be less substitutable. As for the modifiability of a word combination, it can be estimated by two sets of features. The first set characterizes the distribution significance of how two words co-occur at different positions. For example, Spread [Smadja 1993; Sun et al. 1997], bidirectional Spread [Xu et al. 2006], and other features are used to estimate whether

two words co-occur in limited positions or are evenly distributed. Naturally, a strong collocation should not be evenly distributed at many positions. The second set of features is the number of peak co-occurrence [Smadja 1993]. For a word bigram, if the co-occurrence frequency at one position is obviously higher than the average co-occurrence, this bigram is considered to have a peak co-occurrence. If a word bi-gram has only one peak distribution, it is regarded as nonmodifiable, while more than two peak distributions indicates modifiability.

5.   Most collocations are grammatically well-formed. Therefore, parsing and chunking techniques are always applied to test the well formedness of the word combinations. A word combination that has direct syntactic relation or dependency or is within the same chunk naturally has higher probability to be collocated [Lin 1997; Zhou et al. 2001; Wuand Zhou 2003; Lu et al. 2004]. More details on these features will be discussed in Chapter 8.3.

6.   Domain information and documentation distribution are features for estimating domain dependence of a collocation. If one collocation occurred in some domains or documents much more frequently, it is regarded as a domain-dependent collocation. The IR techniques for estimating the word distributions in different documents are effective computational features for this task. Pecina [2005] made a survey on these features.

7.4   CATEGORIZATION

Collocations cover a wide spectrum ranging from idioms to free word combinations. Some collocations are very rigid and some are flexible. There are also collocations that are in between. This is one of the reasons why different collocation definitions were proposed in the literature.

Firth [1957] proposed to categorize collocations into general, usual, restricted technical, and personal collocations. However, he did not give a strict definition and a clear categorization scheme.

Based on the areas of use, recurrence status and sense of words as criteria, Wei [2002] categorized collocations into usual (general), figurative, specialized, and institutionalized collocations.

Based on linguistic properties and co-occurrence statistics of typical collocations, the internal association of a collocation can be estimated by its compositionality, substitutability, modifiability, word order alterability, and statistical significance. Xu et al. [2006] proposed to classify collocations with similar internal association into one of the following four types. It should be noted here that since collocations are language-dependent, the English translations of some examples of Chinese collocations in the following sections are not good collocations in English.

a)   Type 0: Idiomatic collocation

Type 0 collocations are fully noncompositional as their meanings cannot be predicted from the meanings of their components such as 缘木求鱼 (climbing a tree to catch a fish, which is a metaphor for a fruitless endeavour). Most Type 0 collocations are already listed as idioms in a dictionary. Some terms are also Type 0 collocations. For example, the term 蓝/a 牙/n (Blue-tooth) refers to a wireless communication protocol which is completely different from either 蓝 (blue color) or 牙 (tooth). Type 0 collocations must have fixed forms. Their components must be nonsubstitutable and nonmodifiable, allowing no syntactic transformation and no internal lexical variation. Their components cannot be shifted around, added to, or altered. This type of collocations has very strong internal associations and co-occurrence statistics is not important.

b) Type 1: Fixed collocation

Type 1 collocations are very limited in compositionality, and they have fixed forms which is nonsubstitutable and nonmodifiable. For example, the meaning of the collocation 外交/n 豁免 权/n (diplomatic immunity) is not completely different from the meanings of its components，yet there is an additional meaning carried. Thus, this collocation is compositional to a limited extent. None of the words in a Type 1 collocation can be substituted by any other words to retain the same meaning. Also, they do not support order altering. Finally, Type 1 collocations normally have strong co-occurrence significance to support them.

c) Type 2: Strong collocation

Type 2 collocations are also limited in compositionality. They are also substitutable to a very limited extent. In other words, their components can only be substituted by few synonyms, and the newly formed word combinations retain similar meanings. Furthermore, Type 2 collocations allow limited modifier insertion and the order of components must be maintained. Type2 collocations normally have strong statistical support. For example, each word in the collocation 裁减/v 员额/n cannot be substituted by their synonyms and the word order cannot be changed. Meanwhile, a modifier can be inserted in this collocation, giving a new *n*-gram collocation like 裁减/v 军队/n 员 额/n or 裁减/v 政府/n 员额/n. Thus, this collocation is a Type 2 collocation.

d) Type 3: Loose collocation

Type 3 collocations have loose restrictions. They are nearly compositional. Their components may be substituted by some of their synonyms, while the newly formed word combinations retain the same meanings. In other words, more substitutions of components are allowed but the substitution is not free. Type 3 collocations allow modifier insertion and component order alteration. They are also modifiable. Type 3 collocations have weak internal associations, and they must have statisti-

TABLE 7.1: Comparison of different types of collocations

	TYPE 0	TYPE 1	TYPE 2	TYPE 3
Compositionality	No	Very limited	Limited	Nearly yes
Substitutability	No	No	Very limited	Limited
Modifiability	No	No	Very limited	Nearly yes
Statistical significance	Not required	Not required	Required	Strongly required
Internal association	Very strong	Very strong	Strong	Weak

cally significant co-occurrence in order to qualify. Here are some examples: 合法/v 收入/n (lawful income), 正当/v 收入/n (legitimate income), and 合法/v 收益 (lawful profit).

Table 7.1 summarizes the differences among the four types of collocations in terms of compositionality, substitutability, modifiability, and statistical significance.

Most collocations discussed in the existing lexicography research correspond to Type 0 to Type 2 [Benson et al. 1990; Brundage et al. 1992]. They mainly focused on the compositional aspect. In contrast, most existing corpus linguistic research allows looser restrictions. It emphasized statistical co-occurrence significance and limited modifiability. It always identified word combinations that could be collocated, rather than the ones that tended to be collocated. As such, all Type 0 to Type 3 collocations and some grammatical collocations are their targets [Smadja 1993; Lü and Zhou 2004]. Pearce [2001] further took limited substitutability into account, and thus the collocations recognized by him covered Type 0 to Type 2 collocations and part of Type 3.

Each individual characteristic of collocations in terms of compositionality, substitutability, modifiability, and internal association provided more concrete evidence in the collocation extraction. Study has shown that collocation extraction algorithms based on different types of collocation characteristics were more effective than single type [Xu et al. 2006].

7.5   LINGUISTIC RESOURCES

7.5.1   Collocation Dictionary of Modern Chinese Lexical Words

This dictionary [Zhang et al. 1992] is on collocations of Chinese lexical words. The definition of a collocation adopted in this dictionary is the co-occurrence of two or more lexical words within predefined syntactic patterns. This definition is similar to Cowie [1978] and Benson [1990]. Most listed collocations are bigram types.

The dictionary contains about 8,000 entries including single-character verbs and adjectives as well as two-character nouns (mainly abstract nouns), verbs, and adjectives. For each entry, the corresponding collocations are manually extracted from a 30-million-word corpus. In total, about 70,000 collocations are listed in the dictionary.

The collocations are organized according to predefined collocation frameworks. These frameworks describe three-level information of the collocations. The first level is syntactic function level, which records the syntactic function that can be served by the entry word such as subject (labeled 主), predication (labeled 谓), object (labeled 宾), complement (labeled 补), attribute (labeled 定), head (labeled 主), and adverbial modifier (labeled 状). The second level records the POS of collocated words including noun, verb, adjective, adverb, etc., as well as the regular co-occurrence order. The third level is semantic level, which categorized collocated words according to their semantics. Let us take a sample entry in the dictionary: 精神/n (spirit) to illustrate this.

Framework 1	
Level 1: [主]	Means this word serves as the subject
Level 2: ~+verb	Shows that this word can collocate with a verb when serving as a subject. Meanwhile, this word normally occur before the verb.
Level 3:	
Group a: 鼓舞 激励	The sense of this group of collocated words is embrace. The collocated words include 鼓舞 and 激励.
Group b: 来源 来自	The sense of this group is attribute from. The collocated words include 来源 来自.
Framework 2	
Level 1: [中]	Means this word serves as the head
Level 2: adjective+~	Shows that this word can collocate with an adjective and serves as the head. Meanwhile, this word normally occur behind the adjective.
Level 3:	
Group a: 忘我 无私	The sense of this group of collocated words is selfless. The collocated words include 忘我 and 无私

The problem of this resource is that semantic restrictions are not fully considered, which makes many listed collocation syntactic compound words, but they are not true collocations.

7.5.2 Dictionary of Modern Chinese Collocations

This dictionary [Mei 1999] maintains about 6,000 single-character and two-character entries. For each entry, its collocations are first separated by its word sense. Secondly, the collocations are categorized as:

1. [词] new word, which means the entry and its collocates form a new word;
2. [语] new phrase, which means the entry and its collocates form a phrase, i.e., a collocation;
3. [成] idiom, which means the entry and its collocates form a idiom. Normally, this categorization is only applicable to single-character entries.

To illustrate this, let us take an entry in the dictionary, say, 通讯:

1. Sense 1: 利用电讯设备传递消息 (Use telecommunications equipment to transmit messages)
   – [词] 通讯班 (communication squad)
   – [语] 通讯 设备 (communication equipment), 通讯 工具 (communication tool)

2. Sense 2: 报道消息的文章 (Message, News)
   – [词] 通讯社 (News agency)
   – [语] 发 通讯 (send a message), 写 通讯 (write news)

Categorizing collocations according to the senses is essential for many applications, such as using them as the seeds for WSD. The problem of this dictionary is that the restrictions on many listed collocates are loose, i.e., these listed collocations are compound words rather than true collocations. Noticeably, some listed n-gram collocations are, in fact, sentences.

7.5.3 Chinese Collocation Bank

Chinese Collocation Bank [Xu et al. 2006] is developed to provide multiple kinds of linguistic information for collocations including: (1) the collocated words for each given headwords and verification of their co-occurrences in the corpus; (2) distinguishing n-gram and bigram collocations for the headwords; and (3) for bigram collocations, providing their syntactic dependencies and classification of collocation types (see Chapter 7.4). This resource is constructed by following the definition, property, and categorization of collocations which is presented in the above sections.

For example, in line with headword 安全/an (safety), an *n*-gram collocation 生命/n 财产/n 安全/an is identified. In the following sentence, the occurrence of this collocation is annotated as:

- 确保/v [人民/n 群众/n] BNP 的/u [生命/n 财产/n 安全/an] BNP (ensure life and property safety of people)

  <ncolloc observing="安全/an" w1="生命/n" w2="财产/n" w3="安全/an" start_wordid= "w5">
  </ncolloc>

where <ncolloc> indicates an *n*-gram collocation, w1, w2,...wn give the components of the *n*-gram collocation according to the ordinal sequence, and start_wordid indicates the word id of the first component of the *n*-gram collocation.

Since *n*-gram collocation is regarded as a whole, no annotation of the internal syntactic and semantic relations of *n*-gram collocations is provided.

An example Type 3 bigram collocation 确保/v 安全/an occurs in the following sentence; the occurrence of this collocation is annotated as:

- 遵循/v [确保/v 安全/an] BVP 的/u 原则/n (follow the principles for ensuring the safety)

  <bcolloc observing="安全/an" col="确保/v" head="确保/v " type= "3" relation="VO">
  <dependency no="1" observing="安全/an" head="确保/v" head_wordid="w2" modifier="安全/an" modifier_wordid="w3" relation="VO">
  </dependency>
  </bcolloc>

where <bcolloc> indicates a bigram collocation, col is for the collocated word, head indicates the head of an identified collocation, type is the classified collocation type, relation gives the syntactic dependency relations of this bigram collocation, <dependency> indicates an identified dependency, no is the id of identified dependency within current sentence according to ordinal sequence, observing indicates the current observing headword, head indicates the head of the identified word dependency, head_wordid is the word id of the head, modifier indicates the modifier of the identified dependency, and modifier_wordid is the word id of the modifier.

Currently, 23,581 unique bigram collocations and 2,752 unique *n*-gram collocations corresponding to the 3,643 observing headwords are annotated. Furthermore, their occurrences in the corpus have been annotated and verified. The bigram collocations are manually classified into three types. The numbers of annotated Type 0/1 collocations, Type 2 collocations, and Type 3 collocations are 152, 3,982, and 19,447 respectively. The numbers of Type 3 collocations are much more than the other two types as Type 3 collocation is loosely restricted.

The collocation bank differs from the above collocation dictionaries on two points. First, collocation bank focuses on each occurrence of the collocation in the corpus rather than a summarized collocation entry. The verification and annotation of each occurrence of collocations is useful for analyzing the status and context of collocations. Secondly, the collocation bank classifies collocation into four types, according to the strength of internal association. The categorized collocation subset provides more concrete evidence for the collocation study.

7.6   APPLICATIONS

Firth [1957] stated, "a word is characterized by the company it keeps." Thus, to determine the appropriate meaning of a polyseme (i.e., a word/phrase with multiple meanings) in a given context or to identify the appropriate word to fill in a specific context is heavily dependent on the usage of collocations. Collocation is therefore widely employed in many NLP tasks especially for MT, IR, NLG, WSD, and speech recognition. For example:

1. Collocation differs from one language to another. The mappings of collocations between different languages are helpful to MT [Gitsaki et al. 2000], e.g., when translating "strong tea" to Chinese, the desired output is "浓 茶" rather than "烈 茶"; translating "play" in "play piano" to "弹/v" while translating "play" in "play football" to "踢/v".

2. Collocations can be used in NLG systems to ensure naturalness in its output [Manning and Schütze 1999], e.g., it could avoid errors such as "powerful tea" in English or "烈/a茶/n in Chinese. The quality of output of NLG systems is then improved.

3. Collocations can be employed in IR research. The accuracy of retrieval can be improved if the similarity between a user query and a document can be determined based on common collocations (or phrases) instead of common words [Fagan 1989; Mitra et al. 1997]. Collocations can also be applied in cross-language IR [Smadja 1993; Zhou et al. 2001].

4. Collocations can be used in WSD. "One sense per collocation" is currently the most commonly used assumption in WSD research [Yarowsky 1995]. That is, different senses of a word are indicated by its collocations. For example, 打 is a Chinese verb, when collocating with 酱油, its sense is "buy"; when collocating with 球, it means "play"; when collocating with "架", its sense is "fight". Consequently, collocation plays an indispensable role in WSD research. Another application related to WSD is computational lexicography [Church 1989; Sinclair 1995].

5. Collocations can be used to improve the language models in speech recognition. Conventional language models in speech technology are based on such basic linguistic units as words. Language models based on collocation can predict the pronunciations of words more accurately [Stolcke 1997].

7.7 SUMMARY

This chapter presents the basic concept of Chinese collocations. Since the term "collocation" has different definitions in existing literatures and some of them are even subjected to strong debate [Benson 1990; Church et al. 1990; Manning and Schütze 1999], the definitions of collocation was first reviewed in this chapter. This is followed by the introduction of the qualitative and quantitative features of collocations. Collocation categorization schemes are also studied. There are some readily available resources to support research in Chinese collocation research. Several common resources are outlined in the chapter. Finally, the advantages of collocation in practical applications are highlighted.

Based on the aforesaid quantitative features, different approaches for automatic extraction of Chinese collocations will presented in the next chapter.

· · · ·

CHAPTER 8

Automatic Chinese Collocation Extraction

8.1 INTRODUCTION

Collocation knowledge is essential to many NLP applications such as machine translation, IR, NLG, WSD, and speech recognition. However, collocation knowledge cannot be compiled easily into a collocation dictionary. Traditionally, linguists manually identified and compiled collocations from printed text [Sinclair 1995; Mei 1999]. However, the coverage and consistency of manual work were not ideal [Smadja 1993]. Furthermore, manual compilation is impractical for identifying new collocations from large running text. As texts in electronic form are more readily available today, there are a number of reported works on automatic collocation extraction [Choueka et al. 1983; Shimohata et al. 1997; Sun et al. 1997; Yu et al. 2003b].

This chapter surveys the automatic Chinese collocation extraction techniques. Generally speaking, the framework of automatic Chinese collocation extraction technique is similar to other languages and makes use of some special characteristic related to the Chinese language. In particular, the technique is applied to automatically segmented and POS-tagged Chinese word sequences. According to the main discriminative features and candidate-searching strategies employed, most of these works can be generally categorized into three main basic types: the window-based statistical approach, the syntax-based approach, and the semantic-based approach.

Notice that the reference corpus used in this chapter consists of the texts of several newspapers including People's Daily 1994–1998, Beijing Daily 1996, Beijing Youth Daily 1994, and Beijing Evening News1994. All of the texts are segmented and tagged using a well-developed Segmentor and POS tagger [Lu et al. 2004]. The final reference corpus consists of 97 millions words.

8.2 WINDOW-BASED STATISTICAL APPROACH

Considering that collocations are recurrent word combinations, naturally lexical statistics is used as one of the key features to identify collocations. Using a headword as the starting point, its co-occurring words within the context window are retrieved from the corpus as collocation candidates. Window-based approaches then identify the word combinations with significant lexical statistics as collocations. In the existing works, three types of statistical features are adopted. They are the co-occurrence frequency features, co-occurrence distribution features, and context based features. They are, in turn, surveyed in the following subsections.

In this section, the observable window size is set to −5 to +5 words surrounding the head-word. Three words, namely, a noun 资产/n (asset), a verb 竞争/v (compete), and an adjective 安全/a (safe) are selected as example headwords. The numbers of their co-words in the reference corpus are 5,754, 11,648, and 8,764, respectively. Since collocations are language-dependent, the translation of some sample Chinese collocations in this chapter is noted to be not good English collocations.

8.2.1 Co-occurrence Frequency Features

Many computational metrics have been proposed to estimate the significance of co-occurrence frequency. In this subsection, several popularly adopted metrics are discussed.

Absolute frequency. The early work on automatic collocation extraction was surveyed by [Choueka et al. 1983]. Co-occurrence frequency is selected as the discriminative feature. Naturally, if two words occur together frequently, they are deemed collocated words. The top 10 most frequent words co-occurring with the three target Chinese headwords are given in Table 8.1. In the table, the bolded co-words are true collocations.

The design and implementation of this work was clear and simple. However, its performance, in general, was not so good, especially for low-frequency collocations. Furthermore, employing a fixed value of absolute frequency as the discriminative threshold made these systems sensitive to corpus size.

Relative frequency. Shimohata [1999] proposed a method to automatically retrieve *n*-gram collocations by using relative frequency. First, recurrent word strings surrounding the headword are retrieved from the corpus. Second, every two strings, string *i* and string *j*, are examined. Third, these strings are refined through (i) combining string *i* and string *j* when they overlap with *r* adjoining each other and satisfy the relative frequency threshold, or (ii) filtering out string *i* if string *j* subsumes string *i* and satisfies the relative frequency threshold. Similarly, relative frequency is also applied to extract bigram collocations. Table 8.2 gives the co-words with the top relative frequency for the three example headwords.

In this table, most bigrams with the highest relative frequency are not true collocations. The results show that relative frequency is not a good general metric for finding Chinese collocations. Further observation shows that some low-frequency true collocations are extracted. For example, 负债表/n (debit table) occurs in the corpus 20 times and it always co-occurred with 资产/n (asset). Such kind of low-frequency collocations are difficult to be extracted by using absolute frequency as the metric. Li et al. [2005] showed that relative frequency was good in finding low-frequency true collocations.

TABLE 8.1: Collocation extraction: absolute frequency (f)

HEADWORD 资产/N (ASSET)		HEADWORD 竞争/V (COMPETE)		HEADWORD 安全/A (SAFE)	
CO-WORDS	F	CO-WORDS	F	CO-WORDS	F
国有/v (State-owned)	5,818	市场/n (Market)	6,144	生产/v (Manufacture)	2,049
企业/n (Corporate)	2,134	激烈/a (Cut-throat)	3,766	国家/n (Nation)	1,883
管理/v (Manage)	1,854	是/v (Is)	2,252	是/v (Is)	1,127
投资/v (Invest)	1,829	中/v (Hit)	1,937	保证/v (Ensure)	1,101
固定/v (Fixed)	1,717	国际/n (International)	1,702	问题/n (Problem)	974
是/v (Is)	1,174	企业/n (Enterprise)	1,618	保障/v (Guarantee)	872
元/q (Dollar)	1,111	不/d (Not)_	1,614	确保/v (Ensure)	782
评估/v (Estimate)	1,059	中/f (In the middle of)	1,480	为/v (Target)	772
增值/v (Accretion)	952	参与/v (Participate)	1,367	生命/n (Life)	711
经营/v (Operating)	951	能力/n (Capability)	1,356	工作/v (Work)	709

Pointwise mutual information. Church and Hanks [1990] used a correlation-based metric to extract collocations. In their works, two-word pairs that appear together more frequently than expected by chance are regarded as bigram collocations. The pointwise mutual information, borrowed from the definition in information theory domain [Fano 1961], is employed to estimate correlation between word pairs. If two words, w_{head} and w_{co}, have occurrence probabilities of $P(w_{\text{head}})$ and

TABLE 8.2: Collocation extraction: relative frequency (rf)

HEADWORD 资产/N (ASSET)		HEADWORD 竞争/V (COMPETE)		HEADWORD 安全/A (SAFE)	
CO-WORDS	RF	CO-WORDS	RF	CO-WORDS	RF
负债表/n (Debt sheet)	0.500092	分散化/vn (Decentralized)	0.500359	斯考克罗夫特/nr (Name)	0.500122
加济祖林/nr (Name)	0.500083	范米尔特/nr (Name)	0.500359	从事性/d (Be engaged in)	0.500041
损益/n (Gain and loss)	0.500055	同行间/n (Peer)	0.500359	过去/n (Past)	0.500041
核资/vd (Approved)	0.500055	国内化/v (National)	0.500359	七贤镇/j (Location name)	0.50002
于邢镁的/nr (Name)	0.500028	夺目/vn (Excellent)	0.500359	丹哈姆/nr (Name)	0.50002
保值率/n (Maintenance ratio)	0.500028	如林/v (Abundant)	0.500359	佛尔斯/nr (Name)	0.50002
内敛性/n (Introverted nature)	0.500028	威廉·巴尔/nr (Name)	0.500359	保证期/n (Guarantee period)	0.50002
凝固化/an (Concretionary)	0.500028	攻心战/n (Psychological)	0.500359	克霍费尔/nr (Name)	0.50002
凝固化/vn (Concreting)	0.500028	玛氏/nr (Name)	0.500359	分馏器/n (Fractionators)	0.50002
负债率/n (Debt rate)	0.498901	能源业/n (Energy industry)	0.500359	利文斯通/nr (Name)	0.50002

$P(w_{co})$ in the corpus and their co-occurrence probability is $P(w_{head}w_{co})$, then their mutual information $I(w_{head},w_{co})$ is defined as:

$$I(w_{head}, w_{co}) = \log_2 \frac{P(w_{head}w_{co})}{P(w_{head})\,P(w_{co})} = \log_2 \frac{P(w_{head}|w_{co})}{P(w_{head})} \qquad (8.1)$$

Note that $I(w_{head},w_{co}) \gg 0$ means w_{head} and w_{co} are highly related, $I(w_{head},w_{co}) \approx 0$ means w_{head} and w_{co} are nearly independent, and $I(w_{head},w_{co}) \ll 0$ means w_{head} and w_{co} are highly unrelated. Many other English collocation extraction systems are based on mutual information [Hindle 1990].

In Chinese works, Sun et al. [1997] used mutual information to strengthen a developed collocation extraction system that achieved some additional improvements. Table 8.3 gives the co-words with the highest mutual information for the three example headwords.

It can be observed that few co-words with high mutual information value in Table 8.3 are true collocations. It also showed that the 300 co-words with the lowest mutual information value for each headword are mostly noncollocated. This result confirms the point of Manning and Schütze [1999] that mutual information is a good measure of independence values but not a good measure for dependence because the value of dependence is based on the frequency of individual words.

Mean and variance: Z-score. Unlike the metrics above which treat each word combination as an individual case, features based on Z-score are used to estimate the relative significance of some relevant word combinations. Suppose a given headword w_{head} has n co-words and their corresponding co-occurrence frequency are $f(w_{head},w_{co-i})$ for $i=1,\ldots n$. Z-score, notated as z_i, measures the divergence of the occurrence of ith word combination from the average occurrence as defined below:

$$z_i = \frac{f\left(w_{head}, w_{co-i}\right) - \frac{1}{n}\sum_{j=1}^{n} f\left(w_{head}, w_{co-i}\right)}{\sqrt{\frac{1}{n-1}\left[\sum_{i=1}^{n}\left(f\left(w_{head}, w_{co-i}\right) - \frac{1}{n}\sum_{j=1}^{n} f\left(w_{head}, w_{co-j}\right)\right)\right]^2}} \qquad (8.2)$$

A word combination that has a larger value than other combinations means that it is statistically significant.

Rogghe [1973] applied Z-score to English collocation extraction. It was also employed in the *Xtract* system with the name of *strength*, as proposed by Smadja [1993]. For the given example headwords, the co-words with the top 10 Z-scores are the same as the ones in Table 8.1. Since Z-score measures the co-occurrence significance performance of related words, using Z-score as a threshold for collocation extraction is advantageous because it is insensitive to corpus size. Therefore, many Chinese collocation extraction systems adopted Z-score as the co-occurrence frequency estimation metric [Sun et al. 1997; Lu et al. 2003; Xu and Lu 2006]. The achieved performance is

TABLE 8.3: Collocation extraction: mutual information (MI)

HEADWORD 资产/N (ASSET)		HEADWORD 竞争/V (COMPETE)		HEADWORD 安全/A (SAFE)	
CO-WORDS	MI	CO-WORDS	MI	CO-WORDS	MI
负债表/n (Debt sheet)	9.100	克里甘/nr (Name)	8.683	波音七三七/nz (Boeing 737)	13.267
加济祖林/nr (Name)	9.071	反不/nr (Contrary)	8.683	伯杰/nr (Name)	12.267
损益/n (Gain and loss)	9.071	优质品/n (Qualify products)	8.683	周报制/n (Weely system)	12.267
核资/vd (Approved)	9.071	保优汰劣/l (Elimination)	8.683	核武器库/n (Nuclear arsenal)	12.267
于邢镁的/nr (Name)	9.071	倾轧性/d (Conflict)	8.683	三环桥/ns (Location name)	12.267
保值率/n (Maintenance ratio)	9.071	卡伯特/nr (Name)	8.683	优质段/n (Qualify segment)	12.267
内敛性/n (Introverted nature)	9.071	同层/d (Same layer)	8.683	保护层/n (Protective layer)	12.267
凝固化/an (Concretionary)	9.071	巴克斯代尔/nr (Name)	8.683	坎普/nr (Name)	12.267
凝固化/vn (Concreting)	9.07	暗潮/n (Undercurrent)	8.683	基轴/n (Base)	12.267
创业股/n (Venture unit)	9.07	月月红牌/nz (Brand name)	8.683	斯考克罗夫特/nr (Name)	12.267

better shown as compared with mutual information. However, this metric is ineffective for extracting low-frequency collocations.

Hypothesis testing. Hypothesis testing is a well-developed technique in mathematical statistics, which determines the probability that a given hypothesis is true. Now we formulate a null hypothesis that two words do not form a collocation, i.e., each of the words is generated completely independent of the other, thus their chance of coming together is simply the product of their occurrence probabilities. Hypothesis testing technique is applied to test whether the above null hypothesis is true or false. If the null hypothesis is proven false, it means that the co-occurrence of two words is more than by chance, i.e., the words are collocated [Yu et al. 2003b]. Several statistical test techniques for hypothesis testing were reported in previous research, e.g., t-test, χ^2 test, and likelihood ratio.

a) t-Test

Make a null hypothesis that two words, w_{head} and w_{co} are independent, such that:

$$\text{H0}: P(W_{\text{head}}, W_{\text{co}}) = P(W_{\text{head}})P(W_{\text{co}}) \tag{8.3}$$

the value of t-test is calculated as:

$$t = \frac{\bar{x} - \mu}{\sqrt{\sigma^2/N}} \approx \frac{P(w_{\text{head}}w_{\text{co}}) - P(w_{\text{head}})\,P(w_{\text{co}})}{\sqrt{P(w_{\text{head}}w_{\text{co}})/N}} \tag{8.4}$$

where N is the total number of words in the corpus. If the t statistics is large enough, then the null hypothesis could be rejected, which implies that collocation is identified.

Manning and Schütze [1999] gave an example of applying t-test to collocation extraction. Furthermore, Pearce [2002] showed that t-test is effective in collocation extraction in English, and Yu et al. [2003b] used t-test in Chinese collocation extraction. It was noted that the use of the t-test as a statistical test for hypothesis testing has a limitation since t-test assumes that probabilities are approximately normally distributed, which is untrue for natural language cases [Church et al. 1991].

b) Chi-square test (χ^2-test)

χ^2-test has the advantage that it does not require the probabilities to be normally distributed. For a bigram candidate of w_{head} and w_{co}, the following table shows the dependence of their occurrence:

$a = f(w_{\text{head}}, w_{\text{co}})$	$b = f(w_{\text{co}}, \overline{w_{\text{co}}})$	$f(w_{\text{head}}, *)$
$c = f(\overline{w_{\text{head}}}, w_{\text{co}})$	$d = f(\overline{w_{\text{head}}}, \overline{w_{\text{co}}})$	$f(\overline{w_{\text{head}}}, *)$
$f(*, w_{\text{co}})$	$f(*, \overline{w_{\text{co}}})$	N=Total number of words in corpus

For the word pair $w_{\text{head}}w_{\text{co}}$ in a N-word corpus, its χ^2 value is calculated as:

$$\chi^2 = \frac{N(ad - bc)^2}{(a + d)(a + b)(c + d)(b + d)} \qquad (8.5)$$

If the difference between observed and expected frequencies is large, a collocation of w_{head} and w_{co} is identified. Church and Gale [1991], Kilgarriff [1998], Manning and Schütze [1999], and Yu et al. [2003b] employed χ^2-test for collocation extraction in English and Chinese, respectively.

χ^2-test has two obvious advantages. First, it does not require the assumption that the co-occurrences of candidates fulfil normal distribution. Second, it is appropriate for large probabilities, for which the normality assumption of the t-test fails [Manning and Schütze 1999]. However, Snedecor et al. [1989] pointed out that if the total sample size and the expected values were small, the χ^2-test would be inaccurate.

c)   Likelihood ratio

Likelihood ratio is another widely adopted statistical test for hypothesis testing. Blaheta and Johnson [2001] proposed a simplified algorithm of likelihood ratio test. For w_{head} and w_{co}, the log odds ratio was calculated as:

$$\lambda = \log\frac{a/b}{c/d} = \log\frac{ad}{cb} = \log d - \log b - \log c + \log a \qquad (8.6)$$

The candidate word combinations were sorted by values of the log odds ratio, and the ones with the values fulfilling the requirement of threshold were extracted as collocations.

Likelihood ratio also has the advantage that it works well when the data do not fulfil normal distribution and, especially, when the frequency of words is low. Thus, many existing works on collocation extraction used this statistical test in English [Pearce 2002] and Chinese [Zhou et al. 2001; Lü and Zhou 2004].

Yu et al. [2003b] performed an experiment on statistics-based Chinese collocation extraction. Its results showed that the accuracies achieved by χ^2-test and log likelihood ratio (LLR) were normally better than by t-test. The top 10 co-words corresponding to t-test, χ^2-test, and LLR for the three example headwords are illustrated in Table 8.4, respectively.

There are more computational metrics proposed to estimate the co-occurrence frequency significance. Pecina [2005] gave a comprehensive review of these metrics.

TABLE 8.4: Collocation extraction: hypothesis testing

HEADWORD 资产/N (ASSET)			HEADWORD 竞争/V (COMPETE)			HEADWORD 安全/A (SAFE)		
T-TEST	χ²-TEST	LLR	T-TEST	χ²-TEST	LLR	T-TEST	χ²-TEST	LLR
国有/v (State-owned)	国有/v (State-owned)	固定/v (Fixed)	市场/n (Market)	激烈/a (Cut-throat)	市场/n (Market)	生产/v (Manufacture)	保/v (Ensure)	生产/v (Manufacture)
企业/n (Corporate)	固定/v (Fixed)	投资/v (Invest)	激烈/a (Cut-throat)	公平/a (Fair)	激烈/a (Cut-throat)	国家/n (Nation)	财产/n (Property)	国家/n (Nation)
管理/v (Manage)	存量/n (Inventory)	管理/v (Manage)	中/v (Hit)	正当/v (Allowable)	公平/a (Fair)	保证/v (Ensure)	保卫/v (Protect)	保证/v (Ensure)
投资/v (Invest)	无形/b (Virtual)	评估/v (Estimate)	是/v (Is)	市场/n (Market)	参与/v (Participate)	问题/n (Problem)	矿山/n (Mine)	保障/v (Guarantee)
固定/v (Fixed)	增值/v (Accretion)	增值/v (Accretion)	国际/n (International)	参与/v (Participate)	中/v (Hit)	保障/v (Guarantee)	保障/v (Guarantee)	确保/v (Ensure)
评估/v (Estimate)	评估/v (Estimate)	存量/n (Inventory)	企业/n (Enterprise)	平等/a (Fair)	国际/n (International)	确保/v (Ensure)	人身/n (Life)	财产/n (Property)
元/q (Dollar)	保值/v (Maintenance)	无形/b (Virtual)	不/d (Not)	能力/n (Capability)	能力/n (Capability)	是/v (Is)	危及/v (Endanger)	生命/n (Life)
增值/v (Accretion)	盘活/v (Active)	流失/v (Lose)	中/f (In the middle)	日趋/d (Trend to)	正当/v (Allowable)	生命/n (Life)	保证/v (Ensure)	问题/n (Problem)
经营/v (Operating)	重组/v (Re-organize)	经营/v (Operating)	参与/v (Participate)	对手/n (Rival)	企业/n (Enterprise)	工作/v (Work)	生产/v (Manufacture)	交通/n (Traffic)
是/v (Is)	流失/v (Lose)	国有/v (State-owned)	能力/n (Capability)	引入/v (Introduce)	是/v (Is)	财产/n (Property)	行车/v (Traffic)	维护/v (Protect)

TABLE 8.5: Co-occurrence distribution

		−5	−4	−3	−2	−1	+1	+2	+3	+4	+5
安全/a	度汛/v (Flood pass)	0	0	0	0	1	63	0	0	1	0
安全/a	绝对/d (Absolutely)	2	1	1	2	56	1	1	0	1	0
安全/a	发挥/v (Play)	4	1	2	2	1	8	18	11	12	6
安全/a	具有/v (Country-owned)	1	2	10	5	19	11	5	6	2	4
安全/a	特别/d (Especially)	14	14	12	8	4	5	4	2	1	1
安全/a	作/v (Do)	3	2	3	8	0	4	10	15	15	5
安全/a	大/d (Big)	2	1	0	1	0	26	20	6	4	5

8.2.2 Co-occurrence Distribution Features

Another type of discriminative feature is the lexical statistics based on co-occurrence distribution. Table 8.5 gives the co-correct distribution of seven co-cowards of 安全/a (safe) with the same co-occurrence frequency from −5 words to +5 words position.

It can be observed that the first two true collocations have obvious peak co-occurrence. As for the noncollocated co-words, they are generally evenly distributed. It shows that the distribution histograms of collocated words usually have peaks. Therefore, the metrics estimating the co-occurrence distribution has been proposed for finding collocations.

Smadja [1993] introduced Spread, which is the Z-score value for a collocation candidate on its 10 co-occurrence positions, to measure the co-occurrence distribution significance on different positions. The Spread for headword w_{head} and co-occurring words w_{co}, denoted as Spread(w_{head}, w_{co}), is defined as:

$$\text{Spread}(w_{head}, w_{co}) = \frac{1}{10} \sum_{j=-5}^{5} \left[f(w_{head}, w_{co}, j) - \overline{f(w_{head}, w_{co})} \right]^2 \qquad (8.7)$$

where $f(w_{head}, w_{co}, j)$ is the co-occurrence frequency of w_{head} and w_{co} at position j (j from −5 to +5), and $\overline{f(w_{head}, w_{co})}$ is the average co-occurrence frequency at all 10 positions, respectively. The value of Spread(w_{head}, w_{co-i}) ranges from 0 to 1, and a larger value means w_{head} and w_{co-i} trend to co-occur in limited positions. Thus, it has more probability to be a collocation. The experiment conducted in Sun et al. [1997] showed Spread also worked for Chinese collocation extraction. Xu and Lu

TABLE 8.6: Collocation extraction: co-occurrence distribution (spread)		
HEADWORD 资产/N (ASSERT)	**HEADWORD 竞争/V (COMPETE)**	**HEADWORD 安全/A (SAFE)**
国有/v (State-owned)	市场/n (Market)	生产/v (Manufacture)
固定/v (Fixed)	中/f (In the middle)	国家/n (Nation)
投资/v (Invest)	能力/n (Capability)	交通/n (Traffic)
管理/v (Manage)	激烈/a (Cut-throat)	问题/n (Problem)
无形/b (Virtual)	公平/a (Fair)	财产/n (Property)
评估/v (Estimate)	正当/v (Allowable)	欧洲/ns (Europe)
企业/n (Corporate)	不/d (not)	生命/n (Life)
存量/n (Inventory)	国际/n (International)	和平/n (Peace)
流失/v (Lose)	机制/n (Mechanism)	工作/v (Work)
增值/v (Accretion)	参与/v (Participate)	管理/v (Manage)

[2006] revised Spread for Chinese collocation extraction. The revised metric achieved good results. Table 8.6 gives the co-words with the top Spread values for the three example headwords.

The co-occurrence distribution is shown to be a good discriminative feature, especially for fixed collocation because they normally have fewer co-occurrence positions. Meanwhile, further observations in Chinese show that this feature works better for finding collocations for noun than for verbs.

As discussed in Chapter 7.3, peak co-occurrence is another feature for collocation extraction. A word pair always co-occurring on one peak position has higher probability to be collocated. In Chinese, there are three nonlexical auxiliary words, 的/u 地/u 得/u. They are frequently inserted in the adjective–noun, adverb–verb, and verb–adverb collocations, respectively. Thus, many Chinese collocations have two peak distribution, which is different from English.

Another set of features based on co-occurrence distribution is designed by considering the co-occurrence characteristics of combinations of POS. Xu et al. [2006] observed the occurrence of a set of typical Chinese collocations. It shows that the co-occurrence distributions of words with a

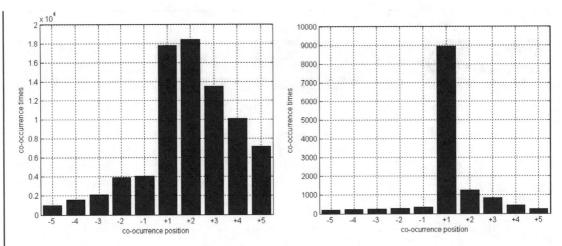

FIGURE 8.1: Co-occurrence distribution of verb–noun and verb–verb collocation.

certain POS combination are similar, yet the distributions of different POS combinations are quite different. Figure 8.1 charts the distributions of verb–noun collocations and verb–verb collocations, respectively. They have shown quite different behaviors.

Xu et al. [2006] considered the use of the POS-related distribution features to produce a new criterion, i.e., the distribution similarity between the candidate and the statistically expected distribution. For bigram $w_{head}w_{co}$, a normalized vector V_{bi} is used to characterize the co-occurrence distribution of $w_{head}w_{co}$. Assume the POS for w_{head} and w_{co} are p_{head} and p_{co}, respectively, another normalized vector V_{pos} is used to characterize the co-occurrence distribution of all of known true collocations between p_{head} and p_{co}, which is regarded as the expected distribution. The production of V_{bi} and V_{pos} measures the similarity between candidate and expected distributions. A larger value means the distribution of the observed bigram candidate is similar to the expected distribution; that is, it tends to be collocated.

8.2.3 Context-Based Features

A collocation is a syntactic and semantic unit. For an uninterrupted collocation, its context normally shows high homogeneity. It means that for each bigram occurring in the corpus, information of its empirical context (frequencies of words occurring within a specified context window) and left and right immediate contexts (frequencies of words immediately preceding or following the bigram) are good criteria for determining whether it is a collocation. By determining the entropy of the immediate contexts of a word sequence, the association measures rank collocations according to the assumption that they occur as units (information theoretically) in a noisy environment [Shimohata

TABLE 8.7: Features based on the entropy of context

NAME	EQUATION
Context entropy	$-\sum_w P\left(w\mid C_{w_{\text{head}},w_{\text{co}}}\right)\log P\left(w\mid C_{w_{\text{head}},w_{\text{co}}}\right)$
Left context entropy	$-\sum_w P\left(w\mid C^{\text{l}}_{w_{\text{head}},w_{\text{co}}}\right)\log P\left(w\mid C^{\text{l}}_{w_{\text{head}},w_{\text{co}}}\right)$
Right context entropy	$-\sum_w P\left(w\mid C^{\text{r}}_{w_{\text{head}},w_{\text{co}}}\right)\log P\left(w\mid C^{\text{r}}_{w_{\text{head}},w_{\text{co}}}\right)$
Left context divergence	$P(w_{\text{head}}*)\log P(w_{\text{head}}*)$ $-\sum_w P\left(w\mid C^{\text{l}}_{w_{\text{head}},w_{\text{co}}}\right)\log P\left(w\mid C^{\text{l}}_{w_{\text{head}},w_{\text{co}}}\right)$
Right context divergence	$P(*w_{\text{co}})\log P(*w_{\text{co}})$ $-\sum_w P\left(w\mid C^{\text{r}}_{w_{\text{head}},w_{\text{co}}}\right)\log P\left(w\mid C^{\text{r}}_{w_{\text{head}},w_{\text{co}}}\right)$

et al. 1997]. By comparing empirical contexts of a word sequence and its components, the association measures rank collocations according to the assumption that semantically noncompositional expressions typically occur in different contexts than their components [Zhai 1997]. Some typical features based on the entropy of context are given in Table 8.7. In this table, C_w is the empirical context of w, $C_{w_{\text{head}},w_{\text{co}}}$ is the empirical context of $w_{\text{head}}w_{\text{co}}$, $C^{\text{l}}_{w_{\text{head}},w_{\text{co}}}$ and $C^{\text{r}}_{w_{\text{head}},w_{\text{co}}}$ are the left and right immediate contexts of $w_{\text{head}}w_{\text{co}}$, respectively.

Normally, only context entropy, left context entropy and right context entropy based on immediate context word are practical to collocation extraction from large corpus. With longer context, the rapidly increased combinations could lead to a large parameter space. Therefore, these features are seldom used for corpus-based collocation extraction.

Another group of context-based features that comes from information theory is mainly based on co-occurrence frequency. Typical ones include cross-entropy which is defined as:

$$-\sum_w P\left(w\mid C_{w_{\text{head}}}\right)\log P\left(w\mid C_{w_{\text{co}}}\right) \tag{8.8}$$

and Euclidean norm is defined as:

$$\sqrt{\sum_w \left[P\left(w\mid C_{w_{\text{head}}}\right)-P\left(w\mid C_{w_{\text{co}}}\right)\right]^2} \tag{8.9}$$

The experiments conducted by Pecina [2005] showed this group of features achieve low accuracy in collocation extraction.

The last group of context-based features comes from the area of IR. Typical features are based on term frequency/inverse document frequency (TF/IDF) which considers the collocation occurrence in different documents. This group of features are mainly designed for recognizing a type of special collocation, i.e., term phrases. They are not applicable to general corpus-based collocation extraction.

Generally speaking, context-based features are designed to recognize uninterrupted collocations. However, their performances in Chinese collocation extraction are not well studied. Note that more context-based features are listed in Appendix B.2 of Pecina's work for reference purposes.

8.2.4 Window Size

Window size is an important parameter in window-based collocation extraction. A large window is effective and helpful for improving recall, but the rapid increased candidates may affect precision. The study on English collocation showed that [−4,+4] or [−5,+5] words was practical for normal and academic English text [Smadja 1993].

The experiments on Chinese collocation extraction showed that [−5,+5] words were also applicable [Sun et al. 1997; Lu et al. 2003]. Furthermore, Sun [1998] observed the distributional property of three-word (one noun, one verb, and one adjective) collocations in a large corpus. The statistics for those collocations showed that the most effective window sizes in collocation extraction were [−2,+1], [−3,+4], and [−1,+2] for noun, verb, and adjective, respectively, in Chinese. However, such result is based on a very small sample space. Thus, the suggested best window size is not convincing. Large-scale statistical analysis on co-occurrence of true collocations is essential for determining optimal size for window-based Chinese collocation extraction.

8.3 SYNTAX-BASED APPROACH

With recent improvement in parsing efficiency and accuracy, syntax and dependency information are employed in collocation extraction approach. This approach emphasizes the characteristics that collocations must be syntactically dependent. Thus, syntactic knowledge can be used to refine collocation candidate searching and filter out some pseudo word combinations. The basic strategy of syntax-based approach is that it restricts collocation candidate searching to word combinations, which match the predefined patterns or has the identified syntactical dependencies, and then identifies the candidates with statistical significance as collocations. The representative works following this approach are introduced below.

TABLE 8.8: POS tag patterns for collocation filtering		
POS PATTERNS	**ENGLISH EXAMPLES**	**CHINESE EXAMPLES**
AN	Linear function	聪明/a 想法/n (Clever idea)
NN	Regression coefficients	国家/n 政策/n (Nation policy)
AAN	Gaussian random variable	公平/a 公开/a 选拔/n (Fair and open election)
ANN	Cumulative distribution function	优惠/a 贷款/n 利率/n (Preferential loan interest)
NAN	Mean squared error	祖国/n 美丽/a 河山/n (Beautiful landscape of homeland)
NNN	Class probability function	国家/n 农业/n 政策/n (Nation agriculture policy)
NPN	Degrees of freedom	N/A

8.3.1   POS Pattern Filter

Justeson and Katz [1995] designed a technique to improve the performance of Choueka's collocation extraction on New York Corpus by filtering out some pseudo collocations. In their work, a set of patterns of consecutive POS tags was used to construct a filter. The candidate phrases, which are output from Choueka's system, were passed through this filter and only the ones matching the POS patterns were let through. In this way, some pseudo collocations were eliminated. The patterns, suggested by Justeson and Katz [1995], are shown in Table 8.8. In this table, each pattern is followed by an example. In those patterns, A refers to an adjective, P a preposition, and N a noun.

The method introduced by Justeson and Katz is simple and effective, and the improved performance of collocation extraction results proves that syntactic information is useful. This method is also applicable to Chinese. Some corresponding Chinese collocation examples are also given in Table 8.8. Although these patterns are effective for finding n-gram collocations, they are not quite effective in finding bigram Chinese collocations.

TABLE 8.9: Types of dependency triples

IDENTIFIERS	RELATIONSHIPS	EXAMPLES	CHINESE EXAMPLES
N:det:D	A noun and its determiner	A dog	匹/d 马/n a (Horse)
N:jnab:A	A noun and its adjectival modifier	Linear function	美丽/a 河山/n (Beautiful landscape)
N:nn:N	A noun and its nominal modifier	Distribution function	国家/n 政策/n (Nation policy)
V:comp1:N	A verb and its noun object	Eat food	打击/v 敌人/n (Attack the enemy)
V:subj:N	A verb and its subject	I have	思想/n 解放/v (Emancipate the mind)
V:jvab:A	A verb and its adverbial modifier	Carefully check	沉重/ad 打击/v (Heavily strike)

8.3.2 Dependency Triple-Based Extraction

Another method is to use dependency parsing to refine candidate searching for collocation extraction in which only the word combinations with identified dependency relations are regarded as candidates. Lin [1997] proposed an English collocation extraction system which is based on dependency parsing. This system achieves broad coverage as well as good precision. In this work, a parser was first employed to extract dependency triples from the text corpus, where a dependency triple consists of a head, a dependency type, and a modifier. The identifiers for the dependency types are outlined in Table 8.9.

The mutual information of these triples was then calculated, and the triples having the values of mutual information greater than a threshold were extracted as collocations. Lin reported that this technique achieved a broader coverage of collocation including low-frequency ones.

Zhou et al. [2001], Wu and Zhou [2003], and Lü and Zhou [2004] reported similar collocation extraction algorithms for Chinese. They used LLR as the statistical metric instead of mutual information. By restricting candidate searching to syntactically dependent triples rather than all context words as done in the window-based approach, the precision of the syntax-based approach was improved [Goldman et al. 2001]. This is because many collocations are interrupted even by long distance, which is difficult for window-based statistical approach. Meanwhile, dependency parsing based extraction can retrieve more low-frequency collocations.

However, the performance of this approach highly relies on the quality and capability of the dependency parser employed. Even for the state-of-art dependency parser, NLPWinParser (Microsoft Corp.), the parsing accuracy on a large corpus is only around 90% [Lü and Zhou 2004]. Parsing errors do propagate to the subsequent collocation extraction stage, thus extraction precision and recall are affected. Secondly, only several typical dependencies can be identified. Therefore, the applicability of this approach is affected. Thirdly, neither the wrong parsing results nor the missed parsing results can be recovered. Thus, the performance of the whole system is affected. Finally, *n*-gram collocation extraction is inappropriate in this method.

8.3.3 Using Chunk Information

Chunking technique is developed to recognize the base phrases in sentences. Since it does not require complex and ambiguous attachment analysis as done in full dependency parsing, chunking method can recognize some local lexical structures at a lower cost and at the same time with higher accuracy. In view of this, Xu and Lu [2005] incorporated chunking information in Chinese collocation extraction.

Based on the observation that chunking relationships between true collocations and pseudo collocations are obviously different, two sets of syntactic patterns with respect to true and pseudo collocations, referred to as support and reject collocation patterns, respectively, are extracted from the training corpus by summarizing the chunking relationships (i.e., a hybrid tag including word POS, chunking status, and head status) corresponding to true and pseudo collocations. Chunking status of each word includes out of a chunk (label O) and at the beginning/in/at the end of a chunk (labelled B/I/E) the syntactic label of chunk [11 chunks including base noun phrase (BNP), base verb phrase (BVP), base adjective phrase (BAP), and so on], and the head information (head of the chunk or not).

The most frequent adjective–noun support collocation patterns are given below. The word bigrams in bold are true collocations matching the support collocation patterns.

1. Support Pattern 1: **a-B-BNP-C n-E-BNP-H** {e.g., [坚强/**a** 后盾/**n**] BNP (solid base)}
2. Support Pattern 2: **a-B-BNP-C** u-I-BNP-C **n-E-BNP-H** {e.g., [必要/**a** 的/u 措施/**n**] BNP (necessary action)}
3. Support Pattern 3: **a-O-O-N** n-B-BNP-C **n-E-BNP-H** {e.g., 重大/**a** [科研/n 成果/**n**] BNP (great research output)}

The most frequent adjective–noun reject collocation patterns are also given below (the word bigrams in bold are not collocations):

1. Reject Pattern 1: **a-B-BNP-C** n-E-BNP-H **n-O-O-N** {e.g., [先进/a 经验/n] BNP 基础/**n** 上/f (based on the advanced experience)}
2. Reject Pattern 2: **a-O-O-N n-B-BNP-C** {e.g., 重大/a [国际/**n** 问题/n] BNP (major world issues)}
3. Reject Pattern 3: **a-O-O-N** u-O-O-N n-B-BNP-C {e.g., 独特/a 的/u [自然/n 景观/n] BNP (the unique nature scenes)}

Xu and Lu [2005] applied the obtained support collocation patterns and reject collocation patterns to improve a statistical-based collocation extraction system by the following two strategies. The first one is to employ support collocation patterns to filter out pseudo collocations in the pre-processing stage. Only if the syntactic relation of a word combination matches one of the support collocation patterns, the combination is kept as input. The second strategy is to use both the support and reject collocation patterns to estimate if certain word combinations are indeed syntactically collocated using probability estimation, and such probabilities are incorporated as an additional feature. The experiments show that both strategies are effective for iimproving statistical-based collocation extraction. Meanwhile, the second strategy has the advantage of avoiding dominating effects caused by syntactic analysis.

8.4   SEMANTIC-BASED APPROACH

Since collocations are semantic-restricted and language-dependent, semantic information is employed to facilitate collocation extraction.

8.4.1   Synonym Substitution Test

Pearsall [2001] proposed a semantic method to improve collocation extraction by using a synonym substitution test. Based on the limited substitutability characteristics that collocations are of customary use and certain collocations can seldom be substituted by other words, not even their synonyms, this technique analyzed the possible substitutions for synonyms among collocation candidates. Once a synonym-substituted word combination occurred in the corpus over a threshold, the original word combination was regarded as grammatically related and was not considered a true collocation. Here, the knowledge recorded in WordNet was used to provide the synonym list.

In Chinese works, Xu et al. [2006] used synonym substitution ratio as the metric for estimating semantic restrictions between collocated words. For example, 晶体/n, 晶/n, 结晶体/n, and

结晶/n (crystal) are a set of synonyms in which only one word 结晶/n frequently co-occurred with 爱情/n (love), thus 爱情/n 结晶/n (love crystal) is a true collocation. On the contrary, 外地/n, 外边/n, 外边/n, 他乡/n, and 外乡 (other places) is another set of synonyms, all of them can compound with 去/v (go); therefore, all these combinations are not true collocations. Li et al. [2004] employed synonym substitution testing with a different strategy. In this approach, synonym substitution of component words in the target Chinese collocations was substituted by their corresponding synonyms. As a result, semantically similar collocations can be determined even if their co-occurrences are physically much lower than their parents.

8.4.2 Translation Testing

Translation testing is another effective method for collocation extraction through estimating the noncompositionality of the candidate collocation. If a word combination cannot be translated word by word into another language, it tends to be noncompositional and hence a true collocation. Manning and Schütze [1999] gave examples showing that some English collocations can be identified by comparing the translation results in French. For example, in a Chinese–English dictionary, 打/v normally means *beat*, *hit*, *strike*, and *spank*. When 打/v co-occurred with 酱油/v (soy sauce), its translation cannot be any of the aforementioned English words. The correct translation is *buy soy sauce*. Hence, 打/v 酱油/v is a true collocation in Chinese.

Furthermore, Wu and Zhou [2003] proposed a method that integrated synonym relationships and context word translation between Chinese and English to automatically acquire synonym collocations in English, and the result was promising. This method is effective in identifying bilingual collocation correspondence such as 订/v 机票/n (book ticket) and 沉重/ad 打击/v (seriously strike).

8.5   CATEGORIZATION-BASED APPROACH

Most collocation extraction algorithms use a single set of criteria and a single threshold. However, this is not appropriate as different types of collocations have different behaviors. Xu and Lu [2006] proposed a categorization-based Chinese collocation extraction system to separately identify different types of collocations (as introduced in Chapter 7) by using different combinations of features. This system incorporates the features from the above three basic approaches and operates in six stages.

The first stage is concordance that builds a bigram co-occurrence table for the headword. In the second stage, statistics-based features incorporating co-occurrence frequency significance and co-occurrence distribution are used to identify bigrams with significant co-occurrence as collocation candidates. The frequently continuously co-occurred bigrams are then extracted as *n*-gram collocations in the third stage. The fourth stage identifies the fixed and strong collocations, i.e., Type 1 and Type 2 collocations. Since Type 1 and Type 2 collocations have strong semantic associations, the synonyms substitution ratio is adopted as one key discriminative feature. Meanwhile, these two types of collocations are narrowly modifiable. Thus, the peak distribution is adopted as another key feature. That is,

1. The value of co-occurrence frequency significance is greater than a threshold.
2. The value of co-occurrence distribution significance is greater than a threshold.
3. The bigram has one peak co-occurrence position, and the occurrence frequency on this position is greater than a threshold.
4. Synonyms substitution ratio for each of the two words is lower than a threshold.

The bigrams satisfying these conditions are extracted as Type 1 and Type 2 collocations. For an example headword 安全/ad (safe), several collocations including 度汛/v (flood pass through) and 运行/v (run) are extracted.

The elimination of pseudo collocations (frequently co-occurred compounds but not true collocations) is difficult by using statistical based extraction techniques only. In the following occurrences of the headword 安全/ad (safely/ad):

- 确保/v 城市/n 安全/ad 度汛/v (ensure the flood pass through the city safely),
- 确保/v 全市/n 安全/ad 度汛/v (ensure the flood pass through the whole city safely),
- 确保/v 三峡/ns 大坝/n 安全/ad 度汛/v (ensure the flood pass through Sanxia Dam safely),

both word combinations {安全/ad, 度汛/v} (safely pass the flood) and {确保/v, 安全/a} (*ensure/v safely/ad*) have strong co-occurrence significance. Yet, only the former is a true collocation. To reduce the pseudo collocations, the use of dependency knowledge is helpful. Xu et al. [2006] proposed 47 heuristic rules based on dependency grammar to remove some bigram co-occurring with identified fixed and strong collocations in the fifth stage. Here are four example rules.

Example Rule 1: For a noun headword, if a verb–noun collocation is identified, all other nouns on the other side of verb window do not collocate with this headword. For example, 保护/v 文物/n (protect cultural relic) is identified as a collocation for headword 文物/n in the sentence:

- 利用/v 新/a 技术/n 保护/v 文物/n (protect cultural relics by using new technology)

The underlined nouns are eliminated from candidates list.

Example Rule 2: For a verb headword, if an adverb–verb collocation is identified, all co-occurrences of other adverbs on the other side of the collocated verb or interrupted by noun/verb on the same side are eliminated. For example, 大力/ad 支持/v (fully support) is identified as a

Type 2 bigram collocation for headword支持/v. Then the underlined adverbs in the following sentence will be eliminated:

- 真诚/ad 感谢/v 大力/**ad** 支持/**v** 和/c 无偿/ad 协助/v (heartfelt thanks for your fully support and volunteer assist)

Example Rule 3: For an adjective headword, if an adjective–noun collocation is identified, all of its other adjective–noun and adjective–verb bigrams within the context windows are discarded. For example, suppose 丑恶/a 嘴脸/n (frightful countenance) is identified as a collocation for headword 丑恶/a in the sentence:

- 揭露/v 奸商/n 的/u丑恶/**a** 嘴脸/**n** (expose the ugly face of profiteers)

The underlined words are not considered as co-words of 丑恶/a and are thus discarded in the consideration of collocations for 丑恶/a.

Example Rule 4: For an adverb headword, if an adverb–verb collocation is identified, the headword will not collocate with any verb on the other side. Thus, all co-occurrences with verbs on the other side are eliminated from the candidate list. For example, 安全/ad 度汛/v (the flood pass through safely) is a collocation for headword安全/ad, thus the underlined verbs could not collocate with 安全/ad in the following examples:

- 确保/v 城市/n 安全/**a** 度汛/**v** (ensure the flood pass through the city safely)

Finally, in the sixth stage, a set of features corresponding to normal collocations, including syntactic distribution similarity, is incorporated with common features such as co-occurrence frequency, co-occurrence distribution, and synonymy substitution rate to identify normal collocations, i.e., Type 3 collocations.

By employing effective strategies to identify different types of collocations in different stages, this system achieves better performance over one-step collocation extraction.

8.6   BENCHMARKS

Currently, there are two benchmarks available for automatic Chinese collocation extraction.

8.6.1   Dictionary of Modern Chinese Collocations (Electronic Version)

"The Dictionary of Modern Chinese Collocation," which is introduced in Chapter 7.5.2, gives some typical collocations for several thousands of headwords [Mei 1999]. The research team in

Hong Kong Polytechnic University analyzed every entry in this dictionary and removed the ones that did not fit the definition of collocation in this book. The co-occurrence statistics of each collocation in the reference corpus is then collected. Only the collocations which occur more than a given threshold are reserved. Finally, a total of 3,643 headwords and their corresponding 35,742 bigram collocations and 6,872 n-gram collocations are obtained.

Most reported works on Chinese collocation extraction evaluated their performance on very few headwords. By adopting this resource, the performance evaluation of Chinese collocation extraction algorithms can be done with a much larger coverage. The resource provides a common ground for comparison of different collocation extraction algorithms.

8.6.2   Collocations for 100 Chinese Headwords

Another answer set is the complete collocation list for more than 100 headwords corresponding to the reference corpus. A number of 134 headwords (47 nouns, 39 verbs, 31 adjectives, and 17 adverbs), whose frequency range from 57 (珍稀/a rare) to 75,987 (关系/n relation), are selected randomly to form a headword set. From all of the word bigrams co-occurring with these headwords, two linguists from our research team have manually identified all true collocations [Xu and Lu 2006]. A number of 4,668 bigram collocations and 935 n-gram collocations are obtained. This collection provides standard answers for evaluating the performance of different collocation extraction algorithms. It is the first attempt to provide a complete collocation list for more than 100 headwords corresponding to a large corpus in Chinese collocation extraction research. By adopting this answer set, both precision and recall of the collocation extraction algorithms can be evaluated while most existing works only reported their precision performance without recall estimation. It means that this answer set can serve as an important resource to support a more objective and all-around performance evaluation on different algorithms.

8.7   SUMMARY

In this chapter, we survey the major approaches for Chinese collocation extraction. These approaches were designed based on different targeting collocation properties. Among them, the window-based statistical approach is the basis of most collocation extraction systems; the co-occurrence frequency significance reflects the recurrent property of collocations, and the co-occurrence distribution significance reflects the limited modifiable property. The syntax-based approach emphasizes that bigram collocations must be syntactically dependent. It is incorporated to refine collocation extraction. The semantic-based approach is developed based on the observations that component words in a collocation can be substituted only by a limited set of similar words. The hybrid categorization-based approach is then discussed. It is shown to be effective and laid the ground for future study in Chinese collocation extraction. Finally, two available benchmarks for evaluation of automatic Chinese collocation extraction are introduced.

APPENDIX A

Linguistics Resources

A.1 PRINTED DICTIONARIES

1. ABC Chinese English Comprehensive Dictionary. University of Hawaii Press.
2. 《现代汉语词典》，中国社会科学院词典编辑室编，商务印书馆，北京.(Modern Chinese Dictionary, 1984.)
3. 《同义词词林》梅家驹、竺一鸣、高蕴琦、殷鸿翔，上海辞书出版社.(Tong Yi Ci Ci Lin, A Chinese Thesaurus 1983.)
4. 《现代汉语实词搭配词典》张寿康、林杏光，商务印书馆. (Collocation Dictionary of Modern Chinese Lexical Words, 2002.)
5. 《现代汉语搭配词典》梅家驹，汉语大词典出版社. (Dictionary of Modern Chinese Collocations, 1999.)

A.2 ELECTRONIC LEXICONS

1. Semantic Dictionary of Contemporary Chinese. Beijing University Center for Chinese Linguistics. http://ccl.pku.edu.cn/ccl_sem_dict/.
2. Chinese–English Name Entity Lists v 1.0. Xinhua News Agency newswire. http://www .ldc.upenn.edu/Catalog/CatalogEntry.jsp?catalogId=LDC2005T34.
3. Chinese–English Translation Lexicon Version 3.0. http://www.ldc.upenn.edu/Catalog/ CatalogEntry.jsp?catalogId=LDC2002L27.

A.3 ELECTRONIC KNOWLEDGE BASE

1. Simplified Chinese. Chinese WordNet. Southeast University and Vrije Universiteit, Amsterdam. http://aturstudio.com/wordnet/windex.php.
2. Traditional Chinese. Chinese WordNet. Academic Sinica in Taiwan. http://cwn.ling .sinica.edu.tw/.
3. Traditional Chinese. Bilingual Ontological WordNet. Academic Sinica in Taiwan. http:// bow.sinica.edu.tw/.
4. Chinese Concept Dictionary. Institute of Computational Linguistics, Peking University. http://icl.pku.edu.cn/icl_groups/ccd.asp.

5. Chinese Word Bank. http://www.cwbbase.com:80/.
6. Electric Expanded Tong Yi Ci Ci Lin (A Chinese Thesaurus). http://ir.hit.edu.cn.
7. Suggested Upper Merged Ontology (SUMO). http://www.ontologyportal.org/.
8. Dong Z, Dong Q. HowNet, A Chinese Knowledge Base. http://www.keenage.com/.
9. FrameNet. University of California at Berkeley. http://framenet.icsi.berkeley.edu./.
10. Chinese Proposition Bank. http://verbs.colorado.edu/chinese/cpb/.
11. LDC Chinese Proposition Bank 1.0/2.0. http://www.ldc.upenn.edu/Catalog/CatalogEntry .jsp?catalogId=LDC2008T07.
12. 搜文解字 - 語文知識網路 (SouWenJieZi—A Linguistic KnowledgeNet). August 1999. http://words.sinica.edu.tw/.
13. *OpenCyc*, A Multi-Contextual Knowledge Base and Inference Engine. Cycorp. http://www.opencyc.org/.

A.4   CORPORA

1. Sinica Balanced Corpus. http://www.sinica.edu.tw/SinicaCorpus/.
2. Text REtrieval Conference (TREC) Corpus. http://www.ldc.upenn.edu/Catalog/Catalog Entry.jsp?catalogId=LDC2000T52.
3. Chinese Gigaword, 2nd ed. http://www.ldc.upenn.edu/Catalog/CatalogEntry.jsp?catalog Id=LDC2005T14.
4. Segmented and POS Tagged Chinese Gigaword, 2nd ed. Academia Sinica, Taiwan. http://www.ldc.upenn.edu/Catalog/CatalogEntry.jsp?catalogId=LDC2007T03.
5. Chinese Gigaword, 3rd ed. http://www.ldc.upenn.edu/Catalog/CatalogEntry.jsp?catalogI d=LDC2007T38.
6. LDC Mandarin Chinese News Text. http://www.ldc.upenn.edu/Catalog/CatalogEntry. jsp?catalogId=LDC95T13.
7. Segmented and POS Tagged People Daily Corpus. Institute of Computational Linguistics, Peking University. http://icl.pku.edu.cn/icl_res/.

A.5   AUTOMATIC SEGMENTOR AND LANGUAGE PROCESSING PLATFORMS

1. Institute of Computing Technology, Chinese Lexical Analysis System (ICTCLAS). http://ictclas.org/.
2. CKIP Segmentor and Parser. Chinese Knowledge Information Processing Group. http://ckipsvr.iis.sinica.edu.tw/.
3. Chinese Natural Language Processing Platform. http://www.nlp.org.cn/.

4. Language Technology Platform (LTP): supporting Chinese word segmentation, POS tagging, named entity recognition, dependency parsing and semantic parsing. Harbin Institute of Technology. http://ir.hit.edu.cn/demo/ltp/.

A.6   TREEBANKS

1. Penn Chinese Treebank 2.0/4.0/ 5.0/6.0. 100,000 words, 325 articles from Xinhua newswire between 1994 and 1998 GB code, with syntactic bracketing. http://www.ldc.upenn.edu/Catalog/CatalogEntry.jsp?catalogId=LDC2001T11, http://www.ldc.upenn.edu/Catalog/CatalogEntry.jsp?catalogId=LDC2004T05, http://www.ldc.upenn.edu/Catalog/CatalogEntry.jsp?catalogId=LDC2005T01, http://www.ldc.upenn.edu/Catalog/CatalogEntry.jsp?catalogId=LDC2007T36.

2. CKIP Tree Bank. http://turing.iis.sinica.edu.tw/treesearch/.

3. Chinese Shallow Treebank and Chinese Chunk Bank. Hong Kong Polytechnic University. http://www4.comp.polyu.edu.hk/~cclab/.

A.7   OTHER TOOLS

1. List of Chinese surnames, character frequency, and Chinese numbers. http://zhongwen.com/.

2. Conversion between GB and Big5, conversion between Unicode and Chinese, Chinese name gender guesser. Chinese Tools. http://www.chinese-tools.com/tools.

References

Allerton DJ. Three or four levels of co-occurrence relations. *Linguistics* 1984; 63: pp. 17–40.

Benson M. Collocations and idioms. In: *Dictionaries, Lexicography and Language Learning.* Oxford: Pergamon Press; 1985.

Benson M. Collocations and general-purpose dictionaries. *International Journal of Lexicography* 1990; 3(1): pp. 23–35. doi:10.1093/ijl/3.1.23

Benson M, Benson E, Ilson R. *The BBI Combinary Dictionary of English: A Guide to Word Combinations.* John Benjamin Publishing Company, 1986.

Blaheta D, Johnson M. Unsupervised learning of multi-word verbs. In: *Proceeding of ACL'01 Workshop on Collocation, July 7, 2001, Toulouse, France.* pp. 54–60.

Brill E. Transformation-based error-driven learning and natural language processing: A case study in part-of-speech tagging. *Computational Linguistics* 1995; 21(4): pp. 543–565 [December].

Brundage et al. *Multiword lexemes: A monolingual and contrastive typology for natural language processing and machine translation.* Technical Report 232 - IBM; 1992.

Carter R. *Vocabulary: Applied Linguistic Perspectives.* London: Routledge; 1987.

Chao YR. *A Grammar of Spoken Chinese.* Berkeley: University of California Press; 1968.

Chen KJ, Chen CJ. Knowledge extraction for identification of Chinese organization names. In: *Proceedings of the Second Workshop on Chinese Language Processing, October 2000, Hong Kong.* pp. 15–21. doi:10.3115/1117769.1117773

Chen KJ, Ma WY. Unknown word extraction for Chinese by a Corpus-based learning method, *International Journal of Computational Linguistics and Chinese Language Processing (IJCPOL)* 1998; 3(1): pp. 27–44.

Chen K, Ma W. Unknown word extraction for Chinese documents. In: *Proceedings of the 19th International Conference on Computational Linguistics (COLING'02), August 24–September 1, 2002, Taipei, Taiwan.* pp. 169–175. doi:10.3115/1072228.1072277

Chen Y, Zeng M. Development of an automated indexing system based on Chinese words segmentation (CWSAIS) and its application. *Journal of Information Science* 1999; 10(5): pp. 352–357. [In Chinese].

Chen C, Bai M, Chen K. Category guessing for Chinese unknown words. In: *Proceedings of Natural Language Processing Pacific Rim Symposium, NLPRS 1997, December 2–4 1997, Phuket, Thailand*. pp. 35–40.

Chen A, Zhou Y, Zhang A, Sun G. Unigram language model for Chinese word segmentation. In: *Proceedings 4th SIGHAN Workshop on Chinese Language Processing, October 14–15, 2005, Jeju Island, Korea*. pp. 138–141.

Cheng KS, Yong GH, Wong KF. A study on word-based and integral-bit Chinese text compression algorithms. *Journal of American Society of Information System (JASIS)* 1999; 50(3): pp. 218–228. doi:10.1002/(SICI)1097-4571(1999)50:3<218::AID-ASI4>3.0.CO;2-1

Chien LF. PAT-tree based adaptive keyphrase extraction for intelligent Chinese information retrieval. *Information Processing and Management* 1999; 35(4): pp. 501–521. doi:10.1016/S0306-4573(98)00054-5

Choueka Y. Looking for needles in a haystack or locating interesting collocation expressions in large textual database. In: *Proceedings of the RIAO'98 Conference on User-Oriented Content-Based Text and Image Handling, March 21–24, 1998, Cambridge, MA*. pp. 21–24.

Choueka Y, Klein T, Neuwitz E. Automatic retrieval of frequent idiomatic and collocational expressions in a large corpus. *ALLC Journal* 1983; 4: pp. 34–38.

Church KW. A stochastic parts program and noun phrase parser for unrestricted text. In: *Proceedings of 2nd Conference on Applied Natural Language Processing, February 9–12, 1988, Austin, TX*. pp. 136–143. doi:10.3115/974235.974260

Church K, Gale W. A comparison of the enhanced Good-Turing and deleted estimation methods for estimating probabilities of English bigrams. *Computer Speech and Language* 1991; 5(1): pp. 19–54. doi:10.1016/0885-2308(91)90016-J

Church KW, Hanks P. Word association norms, mutual information, and lexicography. *Computational Linguistics* 1990; 16(1): pp. 22–29.

Church K, Mercer R. Introduction to the special issue on computational linguistics using large corpora. *Computational Linguistics* 1993: (19); pp. 1–24.

Church KW, et al. Word association, mutual information and lexicography. In: *Proceedings of 27th Annual Meeting of the Association for Computational Linguistics (ACL'89), June 26–29, 1989, University of British Columbia, Vancouver, BC, Canada*. pp. 76–83. doi:10.3115/981623.981633

Church K, et al. Using statistics in lexical analysis. In: Zernik U (ed.), *Lexical Acquisition: Using On-Line Resources to Build a Lexicon*. Hillsdale: Lawrence Erlbaum; 1991. pp. 1–27.

Cowie AP. The place of illustrative material and collocations in the design of a learner's dictionary. In: Strevens P. (ed.), *In Honor of A. S. Hornby*. Oxford: Oxford University Press; 1978. pp. 127–139.

Cowie A, Mackin R. *Oxford Dictionary of Current Idiomatic English*. London: Oxford University Press, 1975.

Cui S, Liu Q, Meng Y, Yu H, Fumihito N. New word detection based on large-scale corpus. *Journal of Computer Research and Development* 2006; 43(5): pp. 927–932. doi:10.1360/crad20060524

DeFrancis J. *The Chinese Language: Facts and Fantasies*. Honolulu: University of Hawaii Press; 1984.

DeFrancis J., et al. *ABC Chinese English Dictionary*. Honolulu: University of Hawaii Press; 2005.

Deng Q, Long Z. A microcomputer retrieval system realizing automatic information indexing. *Journal of Information Science*; 6: pp. 427–432. [In Chinese].

Dictionary 《现代汉语词典》中国社会科学院语言研究所词典编辑室，商务印书馆, 2005.

Dunning T. Accurate methods for the statistics of surprise and coincidence. *Computational Linguistics* 1993; 19(1): pp. 61–74.

Fagan JL. The effectiveness of a non-syntactic approach to automatic phrase indexing for document retrieval. *Journal of the American Society for Information Science* 1989; (40): pp. 115–132.

Fano R. *Transmission of Information*. Cambridge, MA: MIT Press; 1961. pp. 17–23.

Fellbaum C. *WordNet: An Electronic Lexical Database*. Cambridge, MA: MIT Press; 1999.

Fillmore C. Frame semantics. In: *Linguistics in the Morning Calm*. Seoul: Hanshin Publishing Co.; 1982.

Firth JR. Modes of meaning. *Papers in Linguistics 1934–51*. Oxford University Press; 1957. pp. 190–215.

Florian R, Ngai G. Multidimensional transformation-based learning. In: *Proceedings of 5th Workshop on Computational Language Learning (CoNLL01), December 11, 2001, Toulouse, France*. pp. 1–8. doi:10.3115/1117822.1117823

Forney GD. The Viterbi algorithm. *Proc. IEEE* 1973; 61: pp. 268–278. [March].

Friedman T. The World is Flat. April 2005. ISBN 0-374-29288-4.

Fu G. *Research on statistical methods of Chinese syntactic disambiguation*. Doctor Thesis. The Harbin Institute of Technology (HIT), China; 2001.

Fung P. Extracting key terms from Chinese and Japanese texts. *International Journal on Computer Processing of Oriental Language, Special Issue on Information Retrieval and Oriental Languages* 1998; pp. 19–121.

Gale W, Church K, Yarowsky D. A method for disambiguating word senses in a large corpus. *Computers and the Humanities* 1993; 26: pp. 415–439.

Gao W, Wong KF. Experimental studies using statistical algorithms on transliterating phoneme sequences for English–Chinese name translation. *International Journal of Computer Processing of Oriental Language* 2006; 19(1): pp. 63–88.

Gao W, Wong KF, Lam W. Improving transliteration with precise alignment of phoneme chunks and using contextual features. In: *Proceedings of 1ˢᵗ Asia Information Retrieval Symposium (AIRS2004), October 18-20, 2004, Beijing, China*. pp. 63–70.

Gao J, Li M, Wu A, Huang CN. Chinese word segmentation and named entity recognition: A pragmatic approach. *Computational Linguistics* 2005; 31(4): pp. 531–574. [December]. doi: 10.1162/089120105775299177

Ge X, Pratt W., Smyth P. Discovering Chinese words from unsegmented text. In: *Proceedings of the 22nd Annual International ACM SIGIR Conference on Research and Development in Information Retrieval (SIGIR'99), August 15–19, 1999, Berkeley, CA*. pp. 271–272. doi:10.1145/312624.313472

Gitsaki C, et al. *English collocations and their place in the EFL classroom*; 2000. pp. 121–126.

Goldman JP, et al. Collocation extraction using a syntactic parser. In: *Proceedings of 39ᵗʰ Annual Meeting of Association on Computational Linguistics (ACL-0), July 9–11, 2001, Toulouse, France*. pp. 61–66.

Greenbaum S. Some verb-intensifier collocations in American and British English. *American Speech* 1974; (49): pp. 79–89. doi:10.2307/3087920

Halliday MAK. Lexical relations. In: Kress C. (ed.), *System and Function in Language*. Oxford: Oxford University Press; 1976.

Hindle D. Noun classification from predicate argument structures. In: *Proceedings of the 28th Annual Meeting of the Association for Computational Linguistics (ACL-90), June 6–9, 1990, University of Pittsburgh, Pittsburgh, PA*. pp. 268–275. doi:10.3115/981823.981857

Hockenmaier J, Brew C. Error-driven segmentation of Chinese. In: *Proceedings of the 12th Pacific Conference on Language, Information and Communication (PACLIC), February 18–20, 1998, Singapore*. pp. 218–229.

Hoey M. *Patterns of Lexis in Text*. Oxford: Oxford University Press; 1991.

Huang C. Segmentation problem in Chinese processing. *Applied Linguistics* 1997; 1: pp. 72–78. [In Chinese].

Huang C, Zhao H. 中文分词十年回顾. *Journal of Chinese Information Processing* 2007. [In Chinese].

Huang CR, Chen KJ, Chang L, Chen FY. Segmentation standards for Chinese natural language processing. *International Journal of Computational Linguistics and Chinese Language Processing* 1997; 2(2): pp. 47–62.

ICT 2008. http://ictclas.org/

Ide N, Veronis J. Introduction to the special issue on word sense disambiguation: The state of the art. *Computational Linguistic* 1998; 24(1): pp. 1–41.

Internet World Stats. Top Ten Languages Used in the Web. (http://www.internetworldstats.com/stats7.htm).

Jin H, Wong KF. A Chinese dictionary construction algorithm for information retrieval. *ACM Transactions on Asian Language Information Processing*, 2002; 1(4): pp. 281–296. [Dec.]. doi:10.1145/795458.795460

Justeson S, Katz SM. Technical terminology: Some linguistic properties and an algorithm for identification in text. *Natural Language Engineering* 1995; 1: pp. 9–27. doi:10.1017/S1351324900000048

Kang SY, Xu XX, Sun MS. The research on the modern Chinese semantic word formation 《现代汉语语义构词规则初探》. *Journal of Chinese Language and Computing* 2005; 15 (2): pp. 103–112.

康熙字典 (Kangxi Dictionary), 1716.

Kilgarriff A. *Metrics for Corpus Similarity and Homogeneity*. University of Brighton, UK; 1998.

Kjellmer G. Some thoughts on collocational distinctiveness. In: *Corpus Linguistics: Recent Developments in the Use of Computer Corpora in English Language Research*. Costerus N.S.; 1984.

Lafferty J, McCallum A, Pereira, F. Conditional random fields: probabilistic models for segmenting and labeling sequence data. In: *Proceedings of International Conference on Machine Learning (ICML), June 28–July 1, 2001, Williamstown, MA*. pp. 282–289.

Li M, Gao JF, Huang CN, Li JF. Unsupervised training for overlapping ambiguity resolution in Chinese word segmentation. In: *Proceedings of 2nd SIGHAN Workshop on Chinese Language Processing, July 11–12, 2003, Sapporo, Japan*. pp. 1–7. doi:10.3115/1119250.1119251

Li H, Huang CN, Gao J, Fan X. The use of SVM for Chinese new word identification. In: *Proceedings of 1st International Joint Conference on Natural Language Processing (IJCNLP'04), March 22–24, 2004, Hainan, China*. pp. 723–732.

Li WY, et al. Similarity based Chinese synonyms collocation extraction. *International Journal of Computational Linguistics and Chinese Language Processing* 2005; 10(1): pp. 123–144.

Lin DK. Using syntactic dependency as local context to resolve word sense ambiguity. In: *Proceedings of ACL/EACL-97, July 7–12, 1997, Madrid, Spain*. pp. 64–71. doi:10.3115/979617.979626, doi:10.3115/976909.979626

Lin DK. Extracting collocations from text corpora. In: *Proceedings of First Workshop on Computational Terminology, 1998, Montreal*.

Liu Y. New advances in computers and natural language processing in China. *Information Science* 1987; 8: pp. 64–70.

Liu Q, Li S, 基于《知网》的词汇语义相似度计算 (Word similarity computing based on HowNet). *International Journal on Computational Linguistics and Chinese Language Processing* 2002; 7(2); pp. 59-76. [August].

Liu Y, Yu SW, Yu JS. Building a bilingual WordNet-like lexicon: The new approach and algorithms. In: *Proceedings of the 19th International Conference on Computational Linguistics (COLING'02), August 24–September 1, 2002, Taipei, Taiwan*. doi:10.3115/1071884.1071891

Liu J, Liu Y, Yu S. The specification of the Chinese concept dictionary. *Journal of Chinese Language and Computing* 2003; 13(2): pp. 177–194. [In Chinese].

Lu Q, Li Y, Xu R. Improving Xtract for Chinese collocation extraction. In: *Proceedings of IEEE International Conference on Natural Language Processing and Knowledge Engineering, Beijing, China, 2003*. pp. 333–338.

Lu Q, Chan ST, Xu RF, et al. A Unicode based adaptive segmentor. *Journal of Chinese Language and Computing* 2004; 14(3): pp. 221–234.

Lua KT. 《汉字的联想与汉语语义场》, *Communications of COLIPS* 1993; 3(1): pp. 11–30.

Luo Z, Song R. An integrated method for Chinese unknown word extraction. In: *ACL Workshop on Automatic Alignment and Extraction of Bilingual Domain Ontology For Medical Domain Web Search, July 2004, Barcelona, Spain.*

Luo X, Sun MS, Tsou B. Covering ambiguity resolution in Chinese word segmentation based on contextual information. In: *Proceedings of COLING 2002, August 24–September 1, 2002, Taiwan.* pp. 598–604.

Lü, S. Xiandai Hanyu Danshuang Yinjie Wenti Chutan (Preliminary investigation on the mono/disyllabic issue in modern Chinese.) *Zhongguo Yuwen* 1963: pp. 10–22. [in Chinese].

Lü YJ, Zhou M. Collocation translation acquisition using monolingual corpora. In: *Proceedings of the 42nd Annual Meeting of the Association for Computational Linguistics (ACL'04), July 21-26, 2004, Barcelona, Spain.* pp.167–174. doi:10.3115/1218955.1218977

Manning CD, Schütze H. *Foundations of Statistical Natural Language Processing.* MIT Press; 1999.

Martin W, Al B, van Sterkenburg P. On the processing of a text corpus: From textual data to lexicographical information. In: Hartman R (Ed.), *Lexicography, Principles and Practice.* London: Applied Language Studies Series, Academic Press, 1983.

Mckeown R, et al. Collocations. In: Dale R, et al. (Eds.), *A Handbook of Natural Language Processing.* New York: Marcel Dekker; 2000.

Mei JJ. *Dictionary of Modern Chinese Collocations.* Hanyu Dictionary Press, 1999. [In Chinese].

Mei JJ, et al. 梅家驹, 竺一鸣, 高蕴琦, 《同义词词林》,上海辞书出版社, 上海, 1983. (*TongYiCi-CiLin: A Chinese Thesaurus.* Shanghai: Shanghai Dictionary Press; 1983. [in Chinese].)

Miller GA. Introduction to Word-Net: An online lexical database. *International Journal of Lexicography* 1990; pp. 235–244.

Miller GA, Beckwith R, Felbaum C, Gross D, Miller K. *Introduction to WordNet: An On-line Lexical Database.* 1993.

Mitchell TF. *Principles of Firthian Linguistics.* London: Longman Press; 1975.

Mitra M, Buckley C, Singhal A, Cardie C. An analysis of statistical and syntactic phrases. In: *Proceedings of RIAO'97 Conference on Computer-Assisted Searching on the Internet, June 25-27, 1997, Montreal, Quebec, Canada.* pp. 200–214.

MSRA 2008. http://research.microsoft.com/en-us/downloads/7a2bb7ee-35e6-40d7-a3f1-0b743a56b424/default.aspx.

Nie JY, Hannan ML, Jin WY. Unknown word detection and segmentation of Chinese using statistical and heuristic knowledge. *Communication of COLIPS* 1995; 5(1–2): pp. 47–57.

Palmer D, Burger J. Chinese word segmentation and information retrieval. In: *Proceedings of 1997 AAAI Spring Symposium on Cross-Language Text and Speech Retrieval, March 24–26, 1997, Stanford, CA*. pp. 175–178.

Pearce D. Synonymy in collocation extraction. In: *NAACL 2001 Workshop: WordNet and Other Lexical Resources: Applications, Extensions and Customizations, June 3 2001, Carnegie Mellon University*. pp. 41–46.

Pearce D. A comparative evaluation of collocation extraction techniques. In: *Proceedings of 3rd International Conference on Language Resources and Evaluation, May 29–31, 2002, Las Palmas, Spain*. pp. 1530–1536.

Pecina P. An extensive empirical study of collocation extraction methods. In: *Proceedings of the ACL'05 Student Research Workshop, June 27, 2005, Michigan, USA*. pp. 13–18.

Peng F, Schuurmans D. Self-supervised Chinese word segmentation. In: *Proceedings of 4th International Symposium on Intelligent Data Analysis (IDA'01), September 13–15, 2001, Lisbon, Portugal*. pp. 238–247. doi:10.1007/3-540-44816-0_24

Peng F, Feng F, McCallum A. Chinese segmentation and new word detection using conditional random fields. In: *Proceedings of the 20th International Conference on Computational Linguistics (COLING04), August 23–27, 2004, Geneva, Switzerland*. pp. 562–568. doi:10.3115/1220355.1220436

Ponte M, Crof W. Useg: A retargetable word segmentation procedure for information retrieval. In: *Proceedings of 5th Symposium on Document Analysis and Information Retrieval (SDAIR'96), April 15–17, 1996, Las Vegas, USA*.

Rogghe B., The computation of collocations and their relevance to lexical studies. In: *The Computer and Literary Studies*. Edinburgh, NewYork: University Press; 1973. pp. 103–112.

Salton G, Buckley C. Term weighting approaches in automatic text retrieval. *Information Processing and Management* 1988; 24/5: pp. 513–523. doi:10.1016/0306-4573(88)90021-0

Sang ETK, Veenstra J. Representing text chunks. In: *Proceedings of the 9th European Chapter of Association of Computation Linguistics (EACL'99), June 8–12, 1999, Bergen, Belgium*. pp. 173–179. doi:10.3115/977035.977059

Shimohata S. Retrieving domain-specific collocations by co-occurrences and word order constraints. *Computational Intelligence* 1999; 15(2): pp. 92–100. doi:10.1111/0824-7935.00085

Shimohata S, et al. Retrieving collocations by co-occurrences and word order constraints. In: *Proceedings of the 35th Annual Meeting of the ACL and 8th Conference of the EACL, July 7–12,*

1997, Madrid, Spain. pp. 476–481. doi:10.3115/979617.979678, doi:10.3115/976909.979 678

Sinclair J. *Corpus, Concordance, Collocation*. Oxford: Oxford University Press, 1991.

Sinclair J. *Collins COBUILD English Dictionary*. London: Harper Collins.1995.

Smadja F. Retrieving collocations from text: Xtract. *Computational Linguistics* 1993; 19(1): pp. 143–177.

Snedecor et al. *Statistical Methods*. Ames, IA: Iowa State University Press; 1989.

Sproat R, Emerson T. The first international Chinese word segmentation bakeoff. In: *The Second SIGHAN Workshop on Chinese Language Processing, July 2003, Sapporo, Japan*. doi:10.3115/1119250.1119269

Sproat R, Shih C. A statistical method for finding word boundaries in Chinese text. *Computer Processing of Chinese and Oriental Languages* 1990; 4(4): pp. 336–351.

Sproat R, Shih C, Gale W, Chang N. A stochastic finite-state wordsegmentation algorithm for Chinese. *Computational Linguistics* 1996; 22(3): pp. 377–404.

Sornlertlamvanich V, Potipiti T, Charoenporn T. Automatic corpus-based Thai word extraction with the C4.5 learning algorithm. *Proceedings of 18th International Conference on Computational Linguistics (COLING2000), July/Aug. 2000, Saarbrucken, Germany*. pp. 802–807. doi:10.3115/992730.992762

Stolcke A. Linguistic knowledge and empirical methods in speech recognition. *AI Magazine* 1997; 18(4): pp. 25–31.

Sun HL. Distributional properties of Chinese collocations in text. In: *Proceedings of 1998 International Conference on Chinese Information Processing*. Tsinghua University Press; 1998. pp. 230–236.

Sun MS, Fang J, Huang CN. A preliminary study on the quantitative analysis on Chinese collocations. *Chinese Linguistics* 1997; (1): pp. 29–38. [n Chinese].

Sun MS, Shen D, Tsou BK. Chinese word segmentation without using lexicon and hand-crafted training data. In: *Proceedings of the 36th Annual Meeting of the Association for Computational Linguistics and the 17th International Conference on Computational Linguistics (ACL/COLING'98), August 1998, Montreal, Canada*. pp. 1265–1271.

Sun J, Zhou M., Gao J. A class-based language model approach to Chinese named entity identification. *International Journal of Computational Linguistics and Chinese Language Processing* 2003; 8(2): pp. 1–28. [August].

Teahan W, Wen Y, Witten I. A compression-based algorithm for Chinese word segmentation. *Computational Linguistics* 2000; 26(3): pp. 375–393. doi:10.1162/089120100561746

Tseng H. Semantic classification of Chinese unknown words. In: *Proceedings of the 41st Annual Meeting on Association for Computational Linguistics, July 7–12, 2003, Sapporo, Japan*. pp. 72–79. doi:10.3115/1075178.1075188

Tseng H, Chang P, Andrew G, Jurafsky D, Manning C. A conditional random fields word segmenter for SIGHAN bakeoff. In: *Proceedings of the 4th SIGHAN Workshop on Chinese Language Processing, October 14–15, 2005, Jeju Island, Korea.* pp. 168–171.

Uchimoto K, Ma Q, Murata M, Ozaku H, Isahara H. Named entity extraction based on a maximum entropy model and transformational rules. In: *Proceedings of 38th Annual Meeting of the Association for Computational Linguistics (ACL'00), October 3–6, 2000, Hong Kong.* doi:10.3115/1075218.1075260

Vapnik VN. *The Nature of Statistical Learning Theory.* Springer; 1995.

Wang D, Yao T. Using a semi-supervised learning mechanism to recognize Chinese names in unsegmented text. In: *Proceedings of International Conference on Computer Processing of Oriental Languages (ICCPOL'03), August 3–6, 2003, Shenyan, China.*

Wei N. *The Definition and Research System of the Word Collocation.* Shanghai: Shanghai; 2002. [in Chinese].

Wong KF, Lam SS, Lum V. Extracting the inter-word semantic relationship from 《同义词词林》. *International Journal of Computer Processing of Oriental Languages (IJCPOL)* 1997; 10(3): pp. 299–320.

Wu A, Jiang Z. Word segmentation in sentence analysis. In: *Proceedings of 1998 International Conference on Chinese Information Processing, 1998, Beijing, China.* pp. 169–180.

Wu A, Jiang Z. Statistically-enhanced New Word identification in a rule-based Chinese system. In: *Proceedings of the 2nd Chinese Language Processing Workshop, October 7–8, 2000.* pp. 46–51. doi:10.3115/1117769.1117777

Wu W, Tian H. The dictionary method of realizing automatic indexing of scientific and technical documents. *Journal of Information Science;* 7: pp. 97–106. [In Chinese].

Wu Z, Tseng G. Chinese text segmentation for text retrieval: Achievements and problems. *Journal of the American Society for Information Science (JASIS)* 1993. doi:10.1002/(SICI)1097-4571(199310)44:9<532::AID-ASI3>3.0.CO;2-M

Wu F, Zhou M. A comparator for Chinese text information retrieval. In: *Proceedings of 1st International Conference on Computers & Application, 1984, IEEE Computer Society, Beijing.* pp. 37–41.

Wu H, Zhou M. Synonymous collocation extraction using translation information. In: *Proceedings of ACL 2003, July 8–10, 2003.* pp. 120–127. doi:10.3115/1075096.1075112

Wu Y, Zhao J, Xu B. Chinese named entity recognition combining a statistical model with human knowledge. In: *Proceedings of the ACL 2003 Workshop on Multilingual and Mixed-language Named Entity Recognition, July 12, 2003, Sapporo, Japan.* pp. 65–72. doi:10.3115/1119384.1119393

Xia F. The segmentation guidelines for the Penn Chinese Treebank (3.0). Technical Report IRCS Report 00-06, University of Pennsylvania, USA, October 17 2000. (http://www.cis.upenn.edu/~chinese/segguide.3rd.ch.pdf).

Xiao Y, Sun MS, Tsou BK. Preliminary study on resolving covering ambiguities in Chinese word segmentation by contextual information in vector space model. *Computer Engineering and Application (Beijing)* 2001; pp. 87–89.

Xu RF, Lu Q. Collocation extraction with chunking information. In: *Proceedings of IEEE Conference on Natural Language Processing and Knowledge Engineering (NLP-KE'05), October 30–November 1, 2005, Wuhan, China.* pp. 52–57. [Accepted for publication].

Xu RF, Lu Q. A multi-stage collocation extraction system. In: Yeung DS (eds.), *The Advances in Machine Learning and Cybernetics, Lecture Notes on Artificial Intelligences (LNAI 3930). Berlin Heidelberg: Springer-Verlag;* 2006. pp. 740–749. doi:10.1007/11739685_77

Xu RF, Lu Q, Li SJ. The design and construction of a Chinese collocation bank. In: *Proceedings of 5th International Conference on Language Resources and Evaluation, May 24–26, 2006, Genoa, Italy.* 2006.

Xue N. *Defining and Automatically Identifying Words in Chinese.* Ph.D. thesis, University of Delaware, USA, Fall 2001. http://verbs.colorado.edu/~xuen/publications/xue_diss.pdf.

Xue N, Shen L. Chinese word segmentation as LMR tagging. In: *Proceedings of 2nd SIGHAN Workshop on Chinese Language Processing, 2003.* pp. 176–179. doi:10.3115/1119250.1119278

Yarowsky D. Word sense disambiguation using statistical models of Roget's categories trained on large corpora. In: *Proceedings of COLING-92, August 23-28, 1992, Nantes, France.* pp. 454–466.

Yarowsky D. Unsupervised word sense disambiguation rivaling supervised methods. In: *Proceedings 33rd Annual Meeting of the Association for Computational Linguistics (ACL-95), June 26-30, 1995, MIT, Cambridge, MA.* pp. 189–196. doi:10.3115/981658.981684

Yu JS, Yu SW, Liu Y, Zhang HR. Introduction to CCD. In: *Proceedings of International Conference on Chinese Computing (ICCC 2001), November 27–29, 2001, Singapore, 2001a.*

Yu S, Zhu X, Wang H. New progress of the grammatical knowledge-base of contemporary Chinese. *Journal of Chinese Information Processing* 2001b; 15(1): pp. 58–65. [In Chinese].

Yu S, Duan H, Zhu X, Sun B. The basic processing of contemporary Chinese corpus at Peking University specification. *Journal of Chinese Information Processing* 2002: 16(5); pp. 49–64 [16(6); pp. 58–65, In Chinese].

Yu H, Zhang H, Liu Q. Recognition of Chinese organization name based on role tagging. In: *Proceedings of the 20th International Conference on Computer Processing of Oriental Languages, August 3-6, 2003, Shenyang, China;* 2003a. pp. 79–87.

Yu JS, et al. Automatic detection of collocation. In: *Proceedings of 4th Semantic Lexical Semantics Workshop; 2003b.*

Zhai C. Exploiting context to identify lexical atoms: A statistical view of linguistic context. In: *Proceedings of the International and Interdisciplinary Conference on Modeling and Using Context (CONTEXT-97), February 4-6, 1997, Rio de Janeiro, Brasil.* pp. 119–128.

Zhang H., Liu Q. Automatic recognition of Chinese person name based on role tagging. *Chinese Journal of Computer* 2004; 27(1). [In Chinese].

Zhang SK., et al. *Collocation Dictionary of Modern Chinese Lexical Words*. Business Publisher, China, 1992.

Zhang S, Qin Y, Wen J, Wang X. Word segmentation and named entity recognition for SIGHAN Backoff 3. In: *Proceedings of the 3rd SIGHAN Workshop*, 2006. pp. 158–161.

Zhang Q, Hu G, Yue L. Chinese organization entity recognition and association on web pages. In: *Proceedings of the 11th International Conference on Business Information Systems, 5–7 May 2008, Innsbruck, Austria*. pp. 12–23. doi:10.1007/978-3-540-79396-0_2

Zheng J, Tan H, Liu K, Zhao. Automatic recognition of Chinese place names: A statistical and rule-based combined approach. In: *Proceedings of IEEE International Conference on Systems, Man and Cybernetics, 2001*; pp. 2204–2209. [vol. 4].

中华字海 (Zhonghua Zihai Dictionary), 冷玉龙, 韦一心, 中华书局 1994. [in Chinese].

Zhou. 周行健,《现代汉语规范用法大辞典》, 北京: 学苑出版社, 1997.

Zhou M, et al. Improving translation selection with a new translation model trained by independent monolingual corpora. *Computational Linguistics and Chinese Language Processing* 2001; 6(1): pp. 1–26.

Zhou J, Ni B, Chen J. A hybrid approach to Chinese word segmentation around CRFs. In: *Proceedings of the 4th SIGHAN Workshop on Chinese Language Processing, October 14–15, 2005, Jeju Island, Korea*. pp. 196–199.

Author Biographies

Kam-Fai Wong obtained his Ph.D. from Edinburgh University, Scotland, in 1987. At present, he is a professor in the Department of Systems Engineering and Engineering Management, the Chinese University of Hong Kong (CUHK) as well as an adjunct professor of Northeastern University and Peking University, China. His research interest centers on Chinese computing, parallel database and information retrieval. He has published over 200 technical papers in these areas in various international journals and conferences and books. He is the founding Editor-In-Chief of ACM Transactions on Asian Language Processing (TALIP), a co-editor-in-chief of International Journal on Computer Processing of Oriental Languages, and a member of the editorial board of the Journal on Distributed and Parallel Databases, International Journal on Computational Linguistics and Chinese Language Processing and Journal of Chinese Processing (China). He is the conference co-chair of APWeb'08, Shenyang and AIRS'2008, Harbin, China; Program Co-chair of IJCNLP'2005, Jeju, Korea; and panel co-chair of VLDB2002.

Wenjie Li is Assistant Professor in the department of computing at the Hong Kong Polytechnic University, where she has worked since 2001. She received her B.Sc. and M.S. in systems engineering from Tianjing University in 1988 and 1993, respectively, and Ph.D. in information systems from the Chinese University of Hong Kong in 1997. Her main research interests include information extraction, text summarization, natural language processing, and temporal information processing. She has published more than 100 international journal and major conference papers. Currently, she serves as the associate editor of International Journal of Computer Processing of Languages.

Ruifeng Xu is a Research Fellow of Department of Chinese, Translation, and Linguistics at City University of Hong Kong since 2008. He received his B. Eng. from Harbin Institute of Technology and his M. Phil. and Ph.D. in Computer Science from the Hong Kong Polytechnic University. His dissertation and postdoctoral work focused on Chinese collocations. Some outputs are integrated in this book. Xu is currently interested in mining knowledge from text, opinion analysis, and information extraction.

Zheng-sheng Zhang is Associate Professor of Chinese in the Department of Linguistics and Asian/Middle-Eastern Languages at San Diego State University, where he has taught since 1990. He received his B.A. in English language from Capital Normal University in Beijing and M.A. and Ph.D. in Linguistics from Ohio State University. His research interests include Chinese linguistics (tonal phonology, dialectology, functional grammar/discourse analysis, and Chinese writing system), foreign language pedagogy (and the use of technology for language instruction. His current research investigates the patterns of variation in Chinese speech and writing using corpus and statistical methods. He is currently Editor-in-Chief of *The Journal of Chinese Language Teachers' Association*.

Printed in the United States
by Baker & Taylor Publisher Services